Irish

IN MINNESOTA

Ann Regan

Foreword by Bill Holm

 MINNESOTA HISTORICAL SOCIETY PRESS

Cover: John McRaith, Meeker County, 1942

Publication of this book was supported, in part, with funds provided by the June D. Holmquist Publication Endowment Fund of the Minnesota Historical Society.

www.mnhs.org/mhspress

Manufactured in Canada

10 9 8 7 6 5 4 3 2 1

International Standard Book Number: 0-87351-419-X

♾ The paper used in this publication meets the minimum requirements of the American National Standard for Information Sciences Permanence for Printed Library Materials, ANSI Z39.48-1984.

Library of Congress Cataloging-in-Publication Data

Regan, Ann, 1955–
    Irish in Minnesota / Ann Regan ; foreword by Bill Holm.
        p.   cm. — (The people of Minnesota)
    Includes bibliographical references and index.
    ISBN 0-87351-419-X (pbk. : alk. paper)
        1. Irish Americans—Minnesota—History. 2. Irish Americans—Minnesota—
    Saint Paul—History. 3. Minnesota—History. 4. Saint Paul (Minn.)—History.
    5. Minnesota—Ethnic relations. 6. Saint Paul (Minn.)—Ethnic relations. I. Title.
    II. Series.

F615.I6 R44 2002
977.6'0049162—dc21

                                                                            2002016541

This book was designed and set in type by Wendy Holdman, Stanton Publication Services, Saint Paul, Minnesota; and was printed by Friesens, Altona, Manitoba.

Contents

Foreword

by Bill Holm

Human beings have not been clever students at learning any lessons from their three or four thousand odd years of recorded history. We repeat our mistakes from generation to generation with tedious regularity. But we ought to have learned at least one simple truth: that there is no word, no idea that is not a double-edged sword. Take, for example, the adjective *ethnic*. In one direction, it cuts upward, to show us the faces, the lives, the histories of our neighbors and ourselves. It shows us that we are not alone on this planet—that we are all rooted with deep tendrils growing down to our ancestors and the stories of how they came to be not *there,* but *here.* These tendrils are visible in our noses and cheekbones, our middle-aged diseases and discomforts, our food, our religious habits, our celebrations, our manner of grieving, our very names. The fact that here in Minnesota, at any rate, we mostly live together in civil harmony— showing sometimes affectionate curiosity, sometimes puzzled irritation but seldom murderous violence—speaks well for our progress as a community of neighbors, even as members of a civilized human tribe.

But early in this new century in America we have seen the dark blade of the ethnic sword made visible, and it has cut us to the quick. From at least one angle, our national wounds from terrorist attacks are an example of ethnicity gone mad, tribal loyalty whipped to fanatical hysteria, until it turns human beings into monstrous machines of mass murder. Few tribes own a guiltless history in this regard.

The 20th century did not see much progress toward solving the problem of ethnicity. Think of Turk and Armenian, German and Jew, Hutu and Tutsi, Protestant and Catholic, Albanian and Serb, French and Algerian—think of our own lynchings. We all hoped for better from the 21st century but may not get any reprieve at all from the tidal waves of violence and hatred.

As global capitalism breaks down the borders between nation-states, fanatical ethnicity rises to life like a hydra. Cheerful advertisements assure us that we are all a family—wearing the same pants, drinking the same pop, singing and going on line together as we spend. When we invoke *family,* we don't seen to remember well the ancient Greek family tragedies. We need to make not a family but a civil community of neighbors, who may neither spend nor look alike but share a desire for truthful history—an alert curiosity about the stories and the lives of our neighbors and a respect both for difference—and for privacy. We must get the metaphors right; we are neither brothers nor sisters here in Minnesota, nor even cousins. We are neighbors, all us *ethnics,* and that fact imposes on us a stricter obligation than blood and, to the degree to which we live up to it, makes us civilized.

As both Minnesotans and Americans, none of us can escape the fact that we *ethnics,* in historic terms, have hardly settled here for the length of a sneeze. Most of us have barely had time to lose the language of our ancestors or to produce protein-stuffed children half a foot taller than ourselves. What does a mere century or a little better amount to in history? Even the oldest settlers—the almost ur-inhabitants, the Dakota and Ojibwa—emigrated here from elsewhere on the continent. The Jeffers Petroglyphs in southwest Minnesota are probably the oldest evidence we have of any human habitation. They are still and will most likely remain only shadowy tellers of any historic truth about us. Who made this language? History is silent. The only clear facts scholars agree on about these mysterious pictures carved in hard red Sioux quartzite is that they were the work of neither of the current native tribes and can be scientifically dated only between the melting of the last glacier and the arrival of the first European settlers in the territory. They seem very old to the eye. It is good for us, I think, that our history begins not with certainty, but with mystery, cause for wonder rather than warfare.

In 1978, before the first edition of this ethnic survey appeared, a researcher came to Minneota to interview local people for information about the Icelanders. Tiny though their numbers, the Icelanders were a real ethnic group with their own language, history, and habits of mind. They settled in the late 19th century in three small clumps around Minneota. At that time, I could still introduce this researcher to a few old ladies born in Iceland and to a dozen children of immigrants who grew up with English as a second language, thus with thick accents. The old still prayed the Lord's Prayer in Icelandic, to them the language of Jesus himself, and a handful of people could still read the ancient poems and sagas in the leather-covered editions brought as treasures from the old country. But two decades have wiped out that primary source. The first generation is gone, only a few alert and alive in the second, and the third speaks only English—real Americans in hardly a century. What driblets of Icelandic blood remain are mixed with a little of this, a little of that. The old thorny names, so difficult to pronounce, have been respelled, then corrected for sound.

Is this the end of ethnicity? The complete meltdown into history evaporated into global marketing anonymity? I say no. On a late October day, a letter arrives from a housewife in Nevis, Minnesota. She's never met me, but she's been to Iceland now and met unknown cousins she found on an Internet genealogy search. The didactic voice in my books reminds her of her father's voice: "He could've said that. Are we *all* literary?" We've never met, she confesses, but she gives me enough of her family tree to convince me that we might be cousins fifteen generations back. She is descended, she says with pride, from the Icelandic law speaker in 1063, Gunnar the Wise. She knows now that she is not alone in history. She has shadowing names, even dates, in her very cells. She says—with more smug pride—that her vinarterta (an Icelandic immigrant prune cake that is often the last surviving ghost of the old country) is better than any she ate in Iceland. She invites me to sample a piece if I ever get to Nevis. Who says there is no profit and joy in ethnicity? That killjoy has obviously never tasted vinarterta!

I think what is happening in this letter, both psychologically and culturally, happens simultaneously in the lives of hundreds of thousands of Minnesotans and countless millions of Americans. Only the details differ, pilaf, jiaozi, fry bread, collards, latkes, or menudo rather than vinarterta, but the process and the object remain the same. We came to this cold flat place so far from the sea in wave after wave of immigration—filling up the steadily fewer empty places in this vast midsection of a continent—but for all of us, whatever the reason for our arrival: poverty, political upheaval, ambition—we check most of our history, and thus our inner life, at the door of the new world. For a while, old habits and even the language carry on, but by the third generation, history is lost. Yet America's history, much less Minnesota's, is so tiny, so new, so uncertain, so much composed of broken connections—and now of vapid media marketing—that we feel a loneliness for a history that stretches back further into the life of the planet. We want more cousins so that, in the best sense, we can be better neighbors. We can acquire interior weight that will keep us rooted in our new homes. That is why we need to read these essays on the ethnic history of Minnesota. We need to meet those neighbors and listen to new stories.

We need also the concrete underpinning of facts that they provide to give real body to our tribal myths if those myths are not to drift off into nostalgic vapor. Svenskarnas Dag and Santa Lucia Day will not tell us much about the old Sweden that disgorged so many of its poor to Minnesota. At the height of the Vietnam War, an old schoolmate of mine steeled his courage to confess to his stern Swedish father that he was thinking both of conscientious objection and, if that didn't work, escape to Canada. He expected patriotic disdain, even contempt. Instead the upright old man wept and cried, "So soon again!" He had left Sweden early in the century to avoid the compulsory military draft but told that history to none of his children. The history of our arrival here does not lose its nobility by being filled with draft-dodging, tubercular lungs, head lice, poverty, failure. It gains humanity. We are all members of a very big club—and not an exclusive one.

I grew up in western Minnesota surrounded by accents: Icelandic, Norwegian, Swedish, Belgian, Dutch, German, Polish, French Canadian, Irish, even a Yankee or two, a French Jewish doctor, and a Japanese chicken sexer in Dr. Kerr's chicken hatchery. As a boy, I thought that a fair-sized family of nations. Some of those tribes have declined almost to extinction, and new immigrants have come to replace them: Mexican, Somali, Hmong, and Balkan. Relations are sometimes awkward as the old ethnicities bump their aging dispositions against the new, forgetting that their own grandparents spoke English strangely, dressed in odd clothes, and ate foods that astonished and sometimes repulsed their neighbors. History does not cease moving at the exact moment we begin to occupy it comfortably.

I've taught many Laotian students in my freshman English classes at Southwest State University in Marshall. I always assign papers on family history. For many children of the fourth generation, the real stories have evaporated, but for the Hmong, they are very much alive—escape followed by gunfire, swimming the Mekong, a childhood in Thai refugee camps. One student brought a piece of his mother's intricate embroidery to class and translated its symbolic storytelling language for his classmates. Those native-born children of farmers will now be haunted for life by the dark water of the Mekong. Ethnic history is alive and surprisingly well in Minnesota.

Meanwhile the passion for connection—thus a craving for a deeper history—has blossomed grandly in my generation and the new one in front of it. A Canadian professional genealogist at work at an immigrant genealogical center at Hofsos in north Iceland assures me, as fact, that genealogy has surpassed, in raw numbers, both stamp and coin collecting as a hobby. What will it next overtake? Baseball cards? Rock and roll 45 rpms? It's a sport with a future, and these essays on ethnic history are part of the evidence of its success.

I've even bought a little house in Hofsos, thirty miles south of the Arctic Circle where in the endless summer light I watch loads of immigrant descendants from Canada and the United States arrive clutching old brown-tone photos, yellowed letters in languages they don't read, the misspelled name of Grandpa's farm. They feed their information into computers and comb through heavy books, hoping to find the history lost when their ancestors simplified their names at Ellis Island or in Quebec. To be ethnic, somehow, is to be human. Neither can we escape it, nor should we want to. You cannot interest yourself in the lives of your neighbors if you don't take sufficient interest in your own.

Minnesotans often jokingly describe their ethnic backgrounds as "mongrel"—a little of this, a little of that, who knows what? But what a gift to be a mongrel! So many ethnicities and so little time in life to track them down! You will have to read many of these essays to find out who was up to what, when. We should also note that every one of us on this planet is a mongrel, thank God. The mongrel is the strongest and longest lived of dogs—and of humans, too. Only the dead are pure—and then, only in memory, never in fact. Mongrels do not kill each other to maintain the pure ideology of the tribe. They just go on mating, acquiring a richer ethnic history with every passing generation. So I commend this series to you. Let me introduce you to your neighbors. May you find pleasure and wisdom in their company.

Irish

IN MINNESOTA

Father James Coyne set his watch by the regulator clock in Ellestad's jewelry store in Lanesboro, 1910. Coyne, who immigrated from Ireland to Minnesota in 1880, was pastor of St. Patrick's Catholic Church in Lanesboro, where he served for 42 years.

I N THE WINTER OF 1999, Minnesota's newly elected governor, Jesse Ventura, joked on David Letterman's show about St. Paul's crooked streets. "Whoever designed the streets must have been drunk. . . . I think it was those Irish guys. You know what they like to do," he said, making a gesture as if drinking. The studio audience gasped, astounded at the outspoken governor's ethnic slur, and then laughed and applauded. Some of Minnesota's Irish did the same—but others resented the joke or thought it was simply silly.[1]

Their responses show the range of identities that Minnesota's Irish Americans held a hundred years after mass immigration from Ireland had ended. And the various reactions also reflect a history that defies easy generalizations: immigrants and their descendants have created stereotypes and broken them, held to traditions and made new ones. Despite being outnumbered by German immigrants, St. Paul's Irish politicians and priests, maids and seamstresses, dominated the politics and image of the town. Irish farmers, settling on the country's 1850s frontier, built thriving agricultural communities, some of which have maintained themselves for generations, to an extent almost unknown elsewhere in the country. It may be difficult to generalize about the group, but—in grand Irish fashion—Minnesota's Irish Americans have had great fun making and telling stories of their experiences.

Minnesota's immigrant Irish made up only a tiny fraction of the group's total in the United States. From 1870 to its peak in 1890, America's Irish-born population remained above 1,850,000 and lived mostly in the North Atlantic states. But roughly one-eighth of the Irish immigrants (and a good number of their children and grandchildren) lived in the rich farmlands and thriving towns of Illinois, Iowa, Wisconsin, and Minnesota. The Irish-born population of Minnesota was by far the smallest of the four states, averaging only about 10% of the midwestern and 4% of the U.S. totals.[2]

In Minnesota's early years, though, the group was important because of its relatively large size. In 1860 the state's 11,838 Irish-born residents constituted a fifth of its entire foreign-born population. With those born of Irish parents, they made up an eighth of Minnesota's total population—a sizable minority, second only to the Germans. Most lived in southeastern and central Minnesota and the cities of Minneapolis and St. Paul. The masses of arriving German and Scandinavian immigrants, however, soon lowered the Irish

---

The Protestant Irish

This book focuses on the story of the Celtic Irish, who are overwhelmingly members of the Roman Catholic church. But Ireland was colonized for centuries by immigrants from Great Britain, and descendants of these Protestant Irish also emigrated to the United States.

Protestant Irish immigrants to Minnesota are difficult to trace. Many English Anglicans (Episcopalians) and Scots Irish (also known as Ulster Scots) emigrated before the American Revolution, and by the time Minnesota opened for settlement, they had been absorbed into the old-stock American population. But several Scots Irish rose to great prominence in the state, including railroad magnate James J. Hill and Oliver L. Kelley, the founder of the Grange. Scots Irish settlers began arriving in the 1850s, migrating principally from the northern counties of Tyrone, Monaghan, and Cavan. They did not leave because of the Great Famine, which touched them little, but rather as a result of the ensuing changes in land laws, which prohibited further division of farms. Many younger sons, single or recently married, chose to emigrate. They found their way to Minnesota via routes familiar to the Catholic Irish: through New York, with brief stops in Ohio and Illinois, or through eastern Canada, or via New Orleans and the Mississippi River.

The Scots Irish formed identifiable settlements in Hennepin and Todd counties. The first arrivals in the southeastern section of Eden Prairie Township in Hennepin County were members of the Robert Anderson family, who staked claims in 1853 and 1854 and held land for relatives. Like their Irish Catholic contemporaries, they learned to work large acreages, rather than the few intensively cultivated acres that constituted a farm in Ireland.

In 1880 Eden Prairie Township's population of 749 included 264 people of British birth or parentage in 47 households. By far the largest contingent was Scots Irish: 49 Irish born and 192 born in the United States of Irish parents. Thus almost three-quarters of the British and over a fourth of the township was of Irish stock. The families were interrelated: more than half of the British households were represented by nine surnames.

Most of these Scots Irish were uncompromising Presbyterians. (One ardent Orangeman,

---

profile. In 1870 the 21,746 Irish born constituted 13.5% of the foreign born; by 1890, the peak year for the Irish population of Minnesota and the United States, there were 28,011, forming just 6% of the state's total foreign-born population. As political and economic conditions in Ireland improved, emigration to the United States slowed. The aging of Minnesota's first- and second-generation Irish further decreased their numbers. By 1950 only 2,693 natives of Ireland lived in Minnesota; in 1990 there were 619.[3]

Why did so few Irish move west from the eastern seaports where they landed? The reasons are rooted in the conditions of Irish Catholic emigration, an outpouring

who was born in Ireland in 1811 and immigrated after homesteading in Canada, asked "to be buried with orange blossoms on his breast so there would be no question about his loyalties.") At first the closest religious services were offered by the Pond brothers' Dakota mission at Bloomington, a long six miles away. By 1856 the settlers had established their own Presbyterian congregation, which still survives. The Episcopalians also organized and built a church, but it lost members to other denominations and disbanded before the end of the century.

The Todd County Scots Irish community consisted of about a half dozen interrelated families, all of whom were members of a strict Presbyterian sect called Covenanters. Some, especially the adult males, were natives of Scotland or Ireland; others were born in Pennsylvania, Ohio, and Indiana. In 1866, bound together by family relationships and fundamental religious beliefs, they sold their farms in Indiana and moved together to Long Prairie, Round Prairie, and Reynolds townships in Todd County. There they settled among a few French and many old-stock Americans, who referred to the newcomers as the Scotch-Irish Covenanters. The men farmed and also did some logging, surveying, and teaching. Religion continued to be a unifying force, but they did not organize the Round Prairie congregation of the Reformed Presbyterian church until 1873. Because the schoolhouse provided adequate meeting space, they did not build a church. Gradually the children and grandchildren moved away. Many went to the Twin Cities or to the Pacific Northwest, but others moved to Kansas, where there appears to have been a similar settlement. By World War II, only a few descendants of the Scots Irish Covenanters still lived in central Todd County.

After the creation of the Irish Free State in 1922, foreign-born immigrants from Northern Ireland were counted separately. By then, years after the height of emigration, their numbers were small: 1,403, or .0005% of the state's total population in 1930. In 1990, when Americans were first asked to declare their ancestry on census forms, the statistical sample suggested that 52,423 Minnesotans, or 1%, claimed some Scots Irish ancestry.

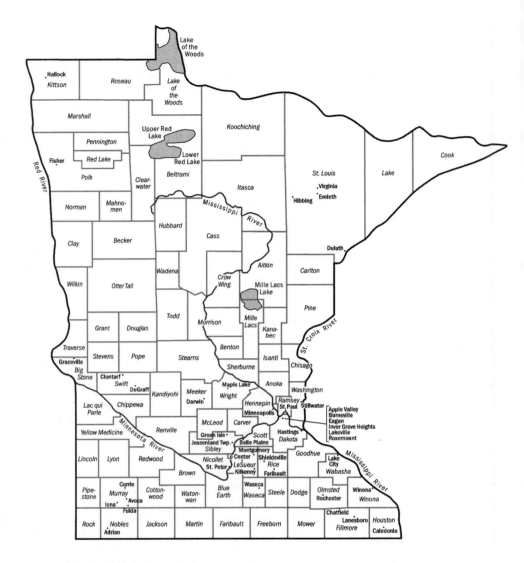

Areas of Irish Settlement in Minnesota

that began in earnest after the War of 1812. Historian Kerby Miller argues that grieving, angry emigrants have forged a litany of hurts and wrongs into a culture of exile—an identity that has caused the Irish to look back at mistreatment, rather than forward to opportunity. Six centuries of English conquest had beaten the Irish into poverty and subjugation. From the 1680s to 1829, the Penal Laws stripped Roman Catholics of various property, civil, and religious rights. For some of these years a bounty was set on the heads of priests, and the faithful held religious services in secret. As 19th-century England modernized and industrialized, its urban population grew; the country became more dependent on Ireland for imports of grain, livestock, and linen—and as a market for its products. Ireland remained agricultural and preindustrial. Overpopulation, excessive land subdivision, grinding poverty, relentless demands for commercial development, high rents, unemployment, agrarian violence, periodic crop failures and typhus epidemics, and political and religious disputes made Ireland a country of little opportunity and great despair.[4]

The failures of the potato crops between 1845 and 1851 added famine to the list of Ireland's troubles and set off mass emigration. A nutritious, high-yielding, and easily tilled vegetable, the potato had supported the country's overwhelmingly agricultural population, had made excessive subdivision possible, and was the dietary mainstay for most of the people. A fungal infection turned the crop to stinking black slime. With its failure, the nation of some 8.5 million shrank to about 6 million by 1855. More than a million people died of starvation and typhus. More than 2.1 million people left Ireland in the greatest proportional population

> **Potato Facts**
>
> In 1845 the potato was virtually the only food for 3.3 million of Ireland's people. Adults consumed between 7 and 15 pounds of potatoes each day, washing them down with buttermilk. This provided virtually all the protein, carbohydrates, and vitamins necessary for a laboring person's diet. Raising such enormous quantities was not difficult: an acre of land would produce six tons of potatoes, more than enough to feed an average family for a year. The failure of the potato crop was devastating.

movement of the 19th century. Almost three-quarters of them emigrated to the United States, an English-speaking nation not under British rule; many others moved to Canada and then crossed the border. Letters and remittances from earlier arrivals established America's reputation for opportunity and high wages, and the first to emigrate then helped finance the trip for relatives who followed.[5]

Although famine brought great numbers of Irish to the United States, only a small proportion of them reached far-off Minnesota, which was part of the agricultural frontier during the crucial decades of this migration. The clichés of Irish immigration—that they were discouraged by their experiences with crop failures, unfamiliar with large-scale farming methods, without capital to invest, and more interested in staying close to countrymen and church—have long been used to explain their preference for low-paying city jobs on the eastern seaboard (where wages were, in fact, six times the rate in Ireland). But the impact of poverty on the massive wave of famine immigrants is undeniable, and the communities near ports of immigration provided the attraction for hundreds of thousands who followed. Yet a significant number of immigrants did earn a stake and then move west.[6]

The Irish were, as historian Lawrence McCaffrey has written, the "pioneers of the American urban ghetto." Characteristics stereotyped as Irish—rough manners, impulsive generosity, ready wit, heavy drinking—offered a defense against, or a respite from, brutal conditions both in Ireland and in American slums. Catholicism, the most prominent symbol of Irish identity and resistance, remained central to Irish American ethnicity. Their "popery" and their continuing intense interest in Ireland's struggle made the immigrant Irish seem especially alien and unassimilable to the unsympathetic Protestant Anglo-American establishment. The mistrust was often mutual. The Irish blamed the British for all of their homeland's troubles, including the famine, and they carried over this prejudice in the form of distrust of that American establishment.

Efforts to lure these immigrants from city slums to farms in the West continually preoccupied Irish leaders in the United States, especially the western clergy, who persuaded some families to move to small Irish settlements in New York, Pennsylvania, Indiana, Illinois, Iowa, and Missouri. But most Irish who migrated west were individuals and families following jobs on building projects, on farms, and in mines in Ohio, Indiana, Illinois, Wisconsin, and Iowa. Other midwestern Irish farmers had left Ireland with capital and purchased land from Yankees who were moving farther west.[7]

It was from states to the east and from Canada that Minnesota drew its early rural Irish settlers. With remarkable consistency, church histories, census records, and individual biographies demonstrate a staged migration: immigrants arrived in New York or Canada and made one or two subsequent moves over a period of years to those states stretching between the East Coast and Minnesota. And people kept moving after reaching Minnesota. From the Irish settlement in and near Faribault, for example, both the original settlers and members of the second generation were attracted to the Twin Cities and to such western states as Washington and California. Small towns across Minnesota also received many members of the second generation.[8]

Early Settlements

Minnesota's earliest Irish arrivals were probably soldiers at Fort Snelling, which was established in 1821 at the confluence of the Minnesota and Mississippi Rivers to assert U.S. control of the lucrative fur trade in the region. By 1838 more than one-fifth of the soldiers stationed at the fort

Lumberjacks of Jim Lane's logging camp, Stillwater, 1887

were Irish immigrants. That year and the next, three of
them—Edward Phelan, John Hays, and William Evans—
were among the first to settle in what became St. Paul. A
German soldier, writing home in 1849, complained about
the Irish: "Then we have many Irish in our company, from
whom we have to bear much; when they are intoxicated,
they knock everything down and want to do nothing but
fight; the guardhouse is always full of them."[9]

The 1850 census found 263 people born in Ireland in
Minnesota Territory, which had been established the year
before. More than one-third of the men were soldiers at
Forts Snelling and Gaines (later renamed Ripley). Many
others were laborers in the new communities growing up
in Dakota, Hennepin, Ramsey, and Washington Counties.
Irish immigrants arriving in New Orleans made their way
up the Mississippi on steamboats that carried goods and
people to the newly opened lands.[10]

Other early arrivals were Irish lumberjacks, who began
arriving in the late 1840s by way of Maine and Canada's

Maritime Provinces. Timber vessels, sailing regularly between Canada and Ireland's shipbuilding ports early in the 19th century, carried immigrants on the westbound voyage. Farmer-lumberers from Maine and New Brunswick, especially from settlements in the latter's Miramichi River Valley, came to the rich timberlands of the St. Croix Valley after the Ojibwe ceded the land in the Treaty of 1837. Stillwater's Irish lumberjack families, often counted as Canadian in the census, built a church in 1853; by 1870 they made Stillwater "a Miramichi town." As the forests were felled, some of the Irish moved north with the logging frontier. Others became craftsmen, small tradesmen, and farmers in and near the area's new towns. A few of the women worked for Yankee families as nursemaids or domestics.[11]

In the 1850s, southeastern Minnesota, especially the counties along the Mississippi and Minnesota Rivers, became home to the first major Irish concentration in the state. Irish farming families in the valleys feeding the Mississippi River may have been attracted to the land by the writings of Mathias Loras, bishop of Dubuque, and his protégé Joseph Cretin, who in 1851 became the first bishop of St. Paul. Loras and Cretin sent letters and articles to the *Boston Pilot* and the *Freeman's Journal* of New York, extolling the opportunities awaiting those who moved west.[12]

The bishops were right. In 1851 the Dakota Indians ceded the rich farmlands west of the Mississippi, which were to be opened to settlement in 1854, after they been surveyed. Would-be farmers did not wait. Immigrants from across the United States and from northern European countries flooded into the land, squatting on claims that they could later prove up. The territory's population jumped from 4,535 in 1850 to more than 150,000 by 1857.[13]

The timing for the Irish was impeccable. As Irish emigrants fled the famine, the western frontier of the new land offered enormous opportunity. Irish laborers could spend

St. Thomas Catholic Church and Cemetery, Jessenland, 1973

a few years digging ditches or building roads, saving the capital that they needed, then take claims on some of the richest land in the country and have a year to earn the cash to pay for it—at $1.25 per acre. The most desirable lands had good soil and the easiest access to transportation. In the early 1850s this meant the Mississippi and Minnesota River valleys. In July 1852 Thomas Doheny, who had immigrated by 1840 and farmed in Pennsylvania, claimed land in what became Jessenland Township on the Minnesota in Sibley County. His first crop—potatoes—was killed by frost, but he and his brothers returned the next year, and they attracted other Irish farmers to the area. Their descendants, still holding the land, claim that this was the first Irish farming community in the state. The settlement at Jessenland soon spread into Green Isle, Washington Lake, and Faxon Townships of Sibley County.[14]

Farmland close to the growing towns of St. Paul and St. Anthony was also in demand. Hennepin County's Irish farmers took land in Corcoran Township and in the Cahill settlement in Richfield Township. The land across the river from St. Paul lacked adequate roads. Territorial boosters in St. Paul and farmers in the new communities, unwilling to wait for a planned military road to St. Peter, contributed in 1853 to the efforts of Captain William B. Dodd, who built a road from St. Paul to St. Peter. Farmers of different ethnicities arrived in droves, traveling down the Dodd Road to areas settled by their countrymen. By 1860 Dakota County had the greatest number of rural Irish, especially in the northwestern townships along the Minnesota River that are now suburbs of the Twin Cities: Burnsville, Eagan, Inver Grove, Lebanon (later Apple Valley), Lakeville, and Rosemount. This concentration extended westward into Scott County, including Glendale, Eagle Creek, Cedar Lake, New

---

A Farmer-Entrepreneur

Michael, Dennis, and Cornelius Callahan immigrated in about 1845 from County Cork to New York, where they worked in the salt mines near Syracuse. In 1849 Michael and his wife, Mary Shea Callahan, moved west to Minnesota, hoping that the climate would restore his health. Their town lot, at Sixth and Wabasha Streets, adjoined the property of Richard Ireland, whose son John would become an archbishop and who eventually bought it. Their farming claim was on the Dodd Road. Michael wrote this letter to Dennis, who had planned to move west as well— but the note was found by his descendents in 1920 in his old log farmhouse near Syracuse. Michael's descendants still live in northern Dakota County.

Saint Paul Sep. 28th /52

Dear Brother I received your letter of 19th on this day which do not place *[please?]* me verry well because I want money very bad. I Bought a town lot here last may and got one year to pay for it and I am Bound to put a house on it and if I am not up to the agreement I will loose all. I expected that I could put up a house on it this fall and rent it house rent is very high here—and then go and live on my claim for the winter which is about 3 miles from this town and 2 of St. peters [Mendota]. I want to have somthing done on it for the spring. I can sell coard wood on the ground but if I had away for hauling it to town I could do well on it. . . . I like this country to live in if I could get good health in it. there is purty good wages a dollar and aquarter a day. . . .

This country is not tried much for farming yet But what I see in it is finest I ever see in america so far as potaties and vegatibiles—

som peoppel fiens fault with the winter being so long. it sat in early last november and went out late in april—if you do come this fall you better buy your flour sugar and coffee and such things in Galena and a cow and a sow-pig. They are very Dear here and if you have money enough Get a yoke of cattle they will cost you about eighty dollars here. . . .

I am sorry that you did not get my lot advertized. There is more than two years since I told you to sel it and if you wanted pay for your trouble there was no one hindren you to take it out of the money when you would sell it—

. . . if you could sell my lot and [then] you do not come put the money in a good bank— get stiffcat of deposit and send it to me there is a company here that will give me the money

No more from your Brother
Michael Callahan

Drinking beer at a house party, Derrynane Township, Le Sueur County, 1910. William Sharkey, the photographer, was a member of the Ancient Order of Hibernians.

Market, and Credit River Townships. Farther up the Minnesota River, early Irish communities included those in Belle Plaine Township of western Scott County, San Francisco and Hollywood Townships of Carver County, and Derrynane and Tyrone Townships of Le Sueur County.[15]

In the Mississippi Valley farther south, smaller Irish farming settlements were located near such villages as Brownsville and Caledonia in Houston County, Chatfield and Lanesboro in Fillmore County, and Rochester in Olmsted County. The valleys of the Zumbro River in Wabasha County and Winnebago Creek in Houston County also held Irish farms. Several river towns such as Winona, Lake City, and Hastings attracted Irish laborers as well as skilled craftsmen during the 1850s and 1860s. The male labor force of Hastings, for example, was one-fifth Irish in 1860.[16]

St. John's choir in Savage, Scott County, 1915. Members: Jim Lannon, Jim Connelly, Walt Dunn, Rose Gallagher, Mary Kennealy, Mag Foley, Julia Foley, Mary Dunn, Bea Dunn.

Main Street, Chatfield, 1901

The Irish population of southeastern Minnesota peaked in 1870 at more than 14,085, which represented almost two-thirds of the state's total Irish-born population that year. More than half (58%) of Minnesota's Irish who were listed as employed in 1870 were farm workers and owners; only Wisconsin and Iowa (also states where farmland was available in these years) had similarly high proportions of Irish farmers. But for the next 40 years, while between 45%

Farm women in Burnsville, Dakota County, about 1944: Mrs. Eli Kearney, Mrs. Jim Kelleher, Mrs. Martin Hayes, Mrs. Tom O'Brien, Mrs. Mike Foley, and Mrs. Frank Gerdermeir

and 57% of Minnesotans worked on farms, the percentage of Irish working on Minnesota farms remained slightly higher, and most of these Irish were listed as farm owners rather than farm laborers.[17]

The state's first organized Irish colony was in Le Sueur and Rice Counties. General James Shields, an Irish-born politician, soldier, lawyer, and entrepreneur, purchased an interest in the townsite of Faribault in 1855 and selected lands in what became Shieldsville and Erin Townships for an Irish Catholic colony. He laid out the townsite of Shieldsville, brought seven Irishmen from St. Paul to settle, and

Kilkenny, 1900. St. Canice Church, named for the cathedral in Kilkenny, Ireland, is at left.

began to promote the colony. By advertising in the Catholic press in states to the east, he attracted Irish farmers who almost filled Shieldsville and Erin as well as parts of Webster and Wheatland Townships. In 1856 St. Patrick's Church was erected at Shieldsville for the 460 Irish-born Catholics in the area. Four years later Rice County had almost 1,200 first- and second-generation Irish, and the Irish had become the predominant group in Faribault.

When the colony spread to Kilkenny and Montgomery Townships in nearby Le Sueur County, the Irish concentration apparently functioned as a community. The 1860 census showed only 93 adult males in Shieldsville Township, but just months earlier 173 votes were cast there in the 1859 congressional election. The losing Republicans protested that "wagonloads of Irish" crossed the line from Le Sueur County to make up the difference.[18]

Teacher John J. Moriarty and the students of the District 44 school, Cleveland Township, Le Sueur County, 1905

Finding Homes across the State

Beginning in the 1850s and especially in the years between 1860 and 1880, the Irish moved west as the frontier shifted into central Minnesota and the upper Minnesota River Valley. Settlements such as Darwin in central Meeker County and Maple Lake in Wright County were started in the 1850s. Birch Cooley Township in Renville County, the Pomme de Terre River region in Stevens County, and Wendel Township in Stearns County attracted some Irish farmers who arrived through Canada after the Dakota War of 1862, as did a section extending across northwestern Stearns and eastern Pope Counties. The Irish populations of the central region reached modest peaks by 1880, when Stearns and Meeker Counties each had

John Vachon, a Farm Security Administration photographer, took pictures on a farm in southeastern Meeker County that was owned by an Irish Catholic family. Jerry McRaith tuned his radio in October 1940; his granddaughter Elaine McCormick made the beds before the arrival of the school bus in February 1942.

nearly 400 Irish-born residents and Wright County had more than 500.[19]

Some of these immigrants had arrived as railroad workers. An 1862 advertisement placed by the St. Paul and Pacific Railroad Company seems to have been directed at recent Irish immigrants: it specified that hands would be paid "nine shillings a day." The Swedes, however, furnished the largest force, with Norwegians, Irish, and Germans joining them in smaller numbers. One contractor preferred "Irishmen for the rock; Swedes, Norwegians &c for the shovel and barrow." After the tracks were laid, some Irish workers in Anoka County bought land near Coon

Knights of Columbus, Assumption of the Blessed Virgin Mary Church, Morris, 1880. Some of the church's Irish parishioners worked in the town's railroad shops.

Creek. Many others took jobs in railroad shops across the state. In 1880, 870 of all the railroad officials and employees in Minnesota were Irish, constituting 6% of the total Irish labor force as well as 14% of the state's railroad employees.[20]

Many of these Irish did not settle in easily identifiable communities. Families from many countries simply settled where they found opportunity, and the Irish, who had the advantage of speaking English, were freer than most. Scores of Catholic churches across the southeastern and central parts of the state listed German, French, and Irish settlers among their founders. The Irish proportion ranged from a family or two to half the congregation. In Paynesville, Stearns County, the Irish and the French cooperated in 1899 to build a church, agreeing that the group selling the most votes at ten cents per ballot would be permitted to choose its name. The total income was $85.00 and the French won: the church was named for St. Louis. But mixed ethnicity could cause problems, especially between Irish and Germans, who resented Irish control of the church hierarchy. And when German Catholics left English-speaking churches to form their own national parishes, the divisions could be painful. In Melrose, Irishmen locked the church door to prevent the Germans from attending.[21]

While thousands of Irish immigrated to Minnesota farmland in the 1850s and 1860s, their numbers were small in comparison to those still living in city ghettos and to the Germans, Norwegians, and Swedes pouring into the Midwest. Western leaders of the Catholic church, like Bishops Loras and Cretin before them, dreamed of similar thriving settlements of Irish Catholics. With a little help, they reasoned, large numbers of Irish farmers could eventually buy land and be as successful as the others. One Minnesota churchman who acted upon this conviction was Bishop John Ireland, the state's leading Irish colonizer, soon to become archbishop of St. Paul.

Born in County Kilkenny in 1838, Ireland emigrated with his family in 1849 and arrived in St. Paul in 1852. He

Archbishop John Ireland, 1908

was ordained in 1861 and served briefly in the Civil War as chaplain of the Fifth Minnesota Regiment, an Irish unit that won fame for its part in the Battle of Corinth. After spending several years as pastor of Cathedral Parish in St. Paul, Ireland became coadjutor bishop in 1875, and he was elevated to archbishop with the creation of the archdiocese of St. Paul in 1888. For the next 30 years he directed the controversial course of the Catholic church in the Northwest and influenced its development in the nation. He believed that Catholic immigrants who seized the opportunities offered by America could establish a truly American church, one that would provide a new model for church-state relations for the European nations that had treated their Catholic citizens so badly. As an enthusiastic supporter of free enterprise, Ireland campaigned for the Republican Party and was a friend of Republican Presidents McKinley, Taft, and Roosevelt. A man of strong opinions, strong will, and unbounded energy—he was dubbed the "consecrated blizzard of the Northwest" by the archbishop of Philadelphia—his importance to the Minnesota Irish and to the history of Minnesota is enormous.[22]

Ireland believed in the Jeffersonian ideal of the yeoman farmer, and he saw how Minnesota's new lands offered that prospect to Irish immigrants. Colonies would swell their numbers. His lieutenant in the colonizing effort was Dillon O'Brien, editor of the weekly diocesan newspaper, the *Northwestern Chronicle,* who used its pages to further such favorite causes as immigration to Minnesota and temperance. Ireland and O'Brien formed the Minnesota Irish Immigration Society in 1864 to promote immigrant aid and colonization programs on a national scale, but little came of these efforts. In 1876, within a month after he became bishop, Ireland tried again, establishing the Catholic Colonization Bureau of St. Paul with O'Brien as its head.[23]

The new bishop avoided problems encountered by other colonizers by becoming an agent of the St. Paul and Pacific Railroad. Because Ireland never bought land from the railroads, he assumed little risk, and he did not need to raise huge amounts of capital to finance the venture. And since he was the sole agent for these tracts, he could prevent speculators from buying up land within the colony and selling it for more than bona fide colonists could afford. Between 1876 and 1879, Ireland contracted for a total of 369,000 acres in southwestern and west-central Minnesota. The towns of De Graff and Clontarf in Swift County, Adrian in Nobles County, Avoca, Iona, and Fulda

Clontarf's first
structure, built in
1876, was the
lumberyard.
Bishop Ireland
asked Dominic
McDermot, an
Irish immigrant,
to be its manager.

in Murray County, Graceville in Big Stone County, and Minneota and Ghent in Lyon County became the business centers for his colonies.[24]

The total number of Irish in these areas was relatively small. In 1870 almost none lived in the counties that were to contain the colonies; by 1880, 1,194 Irish born and 2,087 born in the United States of Irish parents lived there out of a total five-county population of 25,457. The number of foreign-born Irish increased slightly by the turn of the century, but then began to decline. Figures for the second generation do not appear in the census until 1905, when 3,819 persons with Irish-born fathers were recorded.[25]

The Catholic Colonization Bureau did not, however, have the satisfaction of knowing it was saving Irish men and women from the evils of the cities, where jobs were dangerous and housing was unhealthful. Poor laborers did

The Sisters and the Schools

Since 1851, when the first Sisters of St. Joseph arrived in St. Paul, women in religious orders have offered Catholic girls in Minnesota powerful role models. Nuns had careers as teachers, nurses, and administrators, and thousands of girls, a good number of them Irish, joined the eight orders operating in the state. The sisters' largest responsibility was staffing the parochial schools across the state, many of which were established after the 1880s to counter the overtly anti-Catholic curriculum taught in public schools of the time.

While the orders were not segregated by ethnicity, the Sisters of St. Joseph of Carondelet, Missouri—the CSJs—had a strong tradition of Irish leadership in the St. Paul archdiocese. The congregation's Mother Superior for almost 40 years was Mother Seraphine Ireland, John Ireland's sister; her cousin Sister Celestine Howard directed the parochial schools in St. Paul. Across Minnesota and the Dakotas, the CSJs operated 5 hospitals, 3 nursing schools, 12 high schools, and 72 elementary schools. Over the years some 131 women immigrated from Ireland to join the congregation, as did some Irish Canadian women from Prince Edward Island.

The CSJs provided powerful leadership in educating women, including those who would be the next generation of teachers. The College of St. Catherine, opened by the sisters in 1905 in St. Paul, was to become the largest Catholic women's college in the country. Its first dean, Sister Antonia McHugh, was the daughter of Irish immigrants. She pushed her faculty to earn their doctorates by the age of 35 and fought to make St. Catherine's the first accredited Catholic women's college in the region. Struggling to inspire students ("Energize yourself!"), to develop a board of trustees, and to build facilities, Sister Antonia was a natural and successful leader. Her authority was evidently sometimes constrained: after her retirement, she commented to her niece, "Poverty is nothing. Chastity is nothing. But obedience!"

Sister St. Hugh McIver, CSJ, St. Lawrence Catholic School, Minneapolis, 1961

not have the $400 minimum stake needed to see a family through its first year on a western farm. Most of those who took the archbishop up on his offer were, like Irish farmers across the state, from the Midwest and New England. Some were children of farmers in southeastern Minnesota. Others who immigrated directly from Ireland had enough money to pay their passages and expenses for a year. The colonies were largely Irish at first, but French, Belgian, German, and English Catholics also moved to the prairies.[26]

Ireland and O'Brien's colonization scheme offered something valuable to all parties. Settlers bought fertile farms close to churches at reasonable rates. The railroads gained the money from the land sales and customers for their services. The Catholic Colonization Bureau earned the usual agent's fee of 10% on all sales and the satisfaction of seeing Catholic settlers enter the mainstream of American life. The importance of the colonies lies not in the number of Irish they attracted but in their status as the "largest and most successful Catholic colonization program ever undertaken in the United States," as historian James Shannon has described them. There were, however, opponents to Catholic colonization. Church leaders in eastern states did not want to lose members to the colonies, and many actively opposed the effort. And Protestant neighbors and political leaders worried that the "foreignism" of the Catholics would take over the West.[27]

Neither the Catholic bureau nor others were uniformly successful Irish colonizers. The Minnesota Colonization Company, organized in 1877 by William O'Mulcahy, a prominent Irishman from Rochester, failed for lack of financial backing, for the American Irish consistently refused to invest in colonization ventures, preferring to send money to family members in Ireland or to donate to groups working for Irish political and economic reform. Other colonizers found that the experience of the immigrants was vital to the success of a project. Irish families sent with assistance from Boston to the Adrian colony in 1880 were markedly less successful than nonassisted immigrants. So also was a group imported in 1881 from Ireland to a colony near Currie in Murray County by John Sweetman, a wealthy Irishman from County Meath.[28]

To his dismay, Bishop Ireland was himself caught up in a benevolent settlement effort that failed more dramatically than all the rest. In 1880 he accepted responsibility for 309 people from Connemara, County Galway, an area especially hard hit by crop failures, and he placed them on colony land near Graceville in Big Stone County. The winter of 1880–81, which started in mid-October and was the harshest on record, found them unprepared. The colony's Protestant neighbors charged that the church was not supporting the "Connemaras"; other Irish in the colony said the Connemaras were lazy; Ireland's representatives accused the Connemaras of lying about the assistance they had received. Because each of the parties had a deep interest in controlling the story and because the Connemaras themselves spoke Gaelic, it is difficult to evaluate the situation. Newspapers across Minnesota and in the East made a great sensation of the families' suffering. Deeply embarrassed, Ireland found jobs for many of the immigrants with the railroad companies in St. Paul. They lived in a shantytown under Dayton's Bluff on Phalen Creek known as "Connemara Patch," in a similar neighborhood upstream named Swede Hollow, and in other poor neighborhoods on the river flats in Minneapolis and St. Paul.[29]

The failure of the Connemaras had a far greater impact than the incident would seem to warrant. Ireland recognized immediately the consequences of the bad publicity. "The Connemara families are twenty-four in number," he wrote the *St. Paul Pioneer Press*. "Around Graceville are 400 other Catholic families, mostly Irish, and I beg the public, when Graceville is mentioned, to remember the latter rather than the former." Unfortunately for Irish colonization efforts, this was not to be. The story retarded the efforts of at least one recruiter in the East, and it strengthened the stereotype of the Irish as incompetent farmers. It left its mark, too, on the sponsors. Dillon O'Brien's son wrote that the strain of these events contributed to his father's sudden death in 1882. One of Ireland's biographers reported that the archbishop characterized the incident as "the greatest grief of his life."[30]

As the 19th century waned, smaller groups of Irish were to be found farming in the Red River Valley and in the mines and logging camps of northern Minnesota. Kittson County's first Irish settlers migrated from Canada in the 1870s. Tynsid Township near Fisher in Polk County was known as the "Irish Settlement" in 1872 because of its Irish squatters. Others later worked the vast wheat fields of the bonanza farms in summer and the lumber camps of northeastern Minnesota in winter. The St. Paul, Minneapolis, and Manitoba (later the Great Northern) Railroad, built in 1878, brought more Irish laborers. Those working at Hallock attended services in homes from 1879 until 1897,

Potato planters and diggers on a farm in the Red River Valley owned by James J. Hill, 1900

when James J. Hill, the railroad's founder, donated two sections of land and $200 for a church.[31]

Irish immigration to Minnesota had slowed drastically in the 1880s and 1890s, and the Irish born formed only a small part of the labor force in the mines of northern Minnesota's iron ranges. But by 1905 there were more than 1,500 second-generation Irish residents in St. Louis County outside of Duluth, most of them in the range towns. For the first two decades of the 20th century, the Irish, who had the advantage of speaking English, often became the political leaders of the more recently arrived Slavic and Italian miners. Victor L. Power, the son of a Michigan Irish politician, became the first noncompany mayor of Hibbing in 1913. For the next 20 years he taxed the mining companies to finance public improvements that made Hibbing the "richest little village in the world." Other elected officials in Virginia and Eveleth followed suit. Like the Irish politicians in New York's Tammany Hall—and those in Ireland—these men dispensed favors and looked after their own.[32]

Victor L. Power, mayor of Hibbing

"Kelley and his team," Mahoning Mine, Hibbing, 1898

The Erin Go Bragh Saloon, St. Louis Avenue, Minnesota Point, Duluth, 1875

The Irish population of Duluth, the largest city in northern Minnesota, peaked in 1895 with 811 foreign-born Irish residents—3.2% of the city's foreign born—scattered throughout its wards. Of 671 male, Irish-surnamed parishioners at the city's two Irish Catholic parishes in 1892, more than half were laborers; about a quarter worked for the city (as policemen and firemen), in traditional trades such as blacksmithing and printing, or in small businesses. A fifth held white-collar jobs, a few as professionals but most as office workers. Of the 91 Irish-surnamed women working outside the home, 39 were domestics and 26 were dressmakers. The others were employed as office workers, teachers, and laundresses. In 1892 the city's four Ancient Order of Hibernians chapters celebrated St. Patrick's Day with the help of such other Catholic ethnic organizations as the St. Jean Baptiste Society, the Polish National Benevolent Society, and the St. Boniface Society. Duluth's Irish Catholics faced the anti-Catholic prejudice of the American Protective Association from about 1900 to 1918 and of the Ku Klux Klan, which operated in Duluth and on the Iron Range from 1921 to 1927.[33]

After the turn of the century, with the end of large-scale Irish immigration, the declining Irish-born population of the state became progressively more urban. In 1910, three-fifths lived in cities of more than 2,500. But even as their numbers in rural areas fell, Minnesota's Irish departed from the pattern in the United States. In 1920, when 17% of the nation's first- and second-generation Irish lived in rural areas and in towns of less than 2,500, more than twice that proportion—38%—of Minnesota's Irish did so. And the counties of southeastern Minnesota that had shown the highest numbers in 1870 still contained, by 1905, a few hundred Irish born and about a thousand second-generation Irish.[34]

Sullivan and Ryan Wood, Coal and Coke, in 1910, at 591 Rice, St. Paul

St. Paul and Minneapolis

Throughout the state's history, however, the rural Irish received less attention than those concentrated in the Twin Cities, especially in St. Paul. In 1890, when the state's Irish population reached its peak, more than a third of the Irish born lived in the two cities, and three-fifths of these were in St. Paul. Moreover, St. Paul, as the state capital, the center of the Democratic Party for many years, and the seat of a large Catholic archdiocese, became the political, religious, and social center of Irish activity in the state.[35]

The roots of St. Paul's Irish identity are deeply set in the city's economic and social history, and they are part of the story of how the cities came to have such strongly differentiated identities. The Mississippi River gave St. Paul the head of practical navigation and made it the jumping-off point for those going west. Sometimes known as the last city of the East, St. Paul became a railroad town with an economy based on banking, transportation, and the warehouse trade, a population of working-class, Catholic, Democratic residents, and a tradition of cooperation between business and labor. To Minneapolis, the first city of the West, the river gave the Falls of St. Anthony, and thus an economy based on labor-intensive activities such as milling and manufacturing, a class of industrialists whose interests were at odds with their predominantly Scandinavian employees, and a tradition of bitter labor relations. But how St. Paul, with a mainly German population, became an Irish town is a complicated story.[36]

John, William, and Frank Maher, engineers for the Great Northern Railway, 1925. By 1932 the three brothers had together served 146 years on the line.

This characterization grew from modest beginnings. The Irish who migrated to St. Paul in the 1850s found many of the same problems that faced their compatriots in the East. In 1850 more than half of them, a larger proportion than in any other group, were unskilled laborers. "The Catholics are very poor here—and what is worse very irreligious and indifferent," wrote a seminarian in 1852. "They are Half breeds, Canadians, and Irish—The Yankees have all the influence, the wealth and the power, although they are not near as numerous as the others." But even this churchman was not entirely sympathetic: "My mission is among the dirty little ragged Canadian and Irish boys. . . . To take the charge of these impudent and insulting children of unthankful parents was the greatest mortification I ever underwent."[37]

Yankee historians of the time took little notice of the Irish among them, but St. Paul newspapers offer some hints of their activities. The *Minnesota Democrat,* a sympathetic paper, noted on July 15, 1851, that 24 Irishmen donated their labor to construct the first Catholic school in downtown St. Paul. On May 19, 1852, it welcomed "two respectable and intelligent Irish families," who predicted "a considerable immigration of the most substantial class of Irish farmers, within the present season." The *Minnesota Pioneer* reported the first sermon in the Irish language in Minnesota on November 21, 1854.

Other St. Paul newspapers of opposing political views noted more sensational and less flattering activities. The *Daily Minnesotian* was especially interested in Irish voting patterns. In 1857 it reported heavy emigration from Ireland with the comment, "We hope to gracious none of the Paddies will hear where St. Paul is. We consider that those now here can poll a large enough vote, provided they vote often enough apiece." On June 6 of that year the *Minnesota Weekly Times* reported a riot of Irish angered by political defeat in which they "acted as if they were possessed of seven devils apiece." And there were troubles in the neighboring city: the *Minnesota Republican* printed a lively description of a disturbance in Minneapolis on St. Patrick's Day, 1858. The trouble started when pranksters hung St. Patrick in effigy with a string of potatoes around his neck. The editor chastised both the culprits and the Irishmen who took bloody revenge.[38]

The Irish organized early. St. Patrick's Day celebrations began in 1851, and associations such as the St. Patrick's Day Society and the Benevolent Society of the Sons of Erin were formed in the mid-1850s. The Shields Guards, a 52-member volunteer militia organized in 1856 and named for General James Shields, was the Irish answer to the Yankees' Pioneer Guard.[39]

The Fifth Minnesota Regiment

Civil War regiments were often made up of immigrant countrymen. Minnesota's Irish were slower than the Germans to form their own unit, but in December 1861 they began raising troops for the

Fifth Minnesota Regiment. Although they did not completely fill its ranks, the regiment's many Irish soldiers were happy to have the services of Father John Ireland as chaplain. The Fifth Minnesota served in Mississippi, distinguishing itself at the Battle of Corinth by stopping a Confederate charge and allowing Union troops to regroup. The regiment also performed valiantly at Nashville.

Officers of the Fifth Minnesota Regiment: Lucius F. Hubbard, Thomas P. Gere, William B. Gere, and William B. McGrorty

---

St. Paul's Irish spread throughout the city, as the locations of their churches indicated. The first-comers attended the Cathedral of St. Paul with French and German Catholics. Bishop Joseph Cretin, a Frenchman, found it a "strange thing!" that they wished "to celebrate pompously the day of St. Patrick" in 1853, but he was pleased that "No one complains about the sermons in French and English." In 1867 wealthy English-speaking Catholics, several of whom were Irish, built the Church of St. Mary in Lowertown. The next year poorer Irish on the West Side flats, across the Mississippi River from downtown, established St. Michael's Church so that they could attend services without having to pay the toll to cross the bridge. Parishes formed in the following years in middle-class neighborhoods were St. Mark's (organized in 1877 and built in 1889 near the new St. Thomas Seminary on Dayton Avenue), St. Patrick's (built in 1884 near the railroad yards of upper Payne Avenue), St. John's (built in 1886 on Dayton's Bluff and attended by some of the Graceville Connemaras), and St. Vincent de Paul (built in 1888 at 651 Virginia). All had identifiably Irish parishioners, but as the city grew, they acquired more mixed ethnic memberships.[40]

In 1895 the Irish born made up between 3% and 5% of most of St. Paul's wards, with the neighborhoods near downtown holding the largest numbers. By 1930, however, a diminished Irish population was more likely to live in the western parts of the city.[41]

Irish neighborhoods in Minneapolis showed more distinct changes. In 1880 three churches near the city center served Irish congregations: Immaculate Conception, built in 1868 at 3rd Avenue and 3rd Street North; St. Anthony, built in St. Anthony for French Catholics but taken over by Irish (many of whom were stonecutters and quarrymen) and other English speakers in the 1860s; and Holy Rosary, organized in 1878 for Irish railroad workers at Cedar and Riverside. Two-thirds of the Irish-born population of the city lived within six blocks of these three churches, but the areas were so split by ward boundaries that they did not show up as a sizable minority in any one ward. By 1905 there had been some movement north and south out of the downtown area. St. Anthony Church in northeast Minneapolis, however, remained at the center of a strong community. In the next 25 years the Irish-born population shifted south, so that by 1934 two-thirds lived in south Minneapolis.[42]

Changing neighborhoods in Minneapolis reflected shifts in the group's occupational status. In 1880 Irish-born workers held disproportionately high percentages of jobs as laborers, blacksmiths, masons, and stonecutters; hotel, boardinghouse, and restaurant owners and employees; launderers; and civil servants. By 1905 more first- and second-generation Irish worked as clerks, teachers, and salespeople. The changes were dramatic. In 1880 almost two-fifths of those living in households of Irish born were laborers; by 1905 less than a fifth were. Clerical workers and civil servants increased from 7.5% of the Irish labor force in 1880 to 25% in 1905.[43]

Patterns in St. Paul were similar. In 1880, more than two-fifths of the Irish were laborers, twice the city's average.

Regan Brothers Company parked its fleet of delivery trucks near its wholesale bakery at 5th Street and 7th Avenue North, Minneapolis, 1924.

About a third of the Irish-born workers were craftsmen, foremen, and skilled laborers in 1880 and 1890; the same proportion of the first and second generations held these jobs in 1900, roughly equaling the citywide average for such occupations. The Irish were especially well represented in 1880 among boardinghouse keepers, launderers, express company employees, and masons. By 1900 they had gained more positions as clerks, watchmen, firemen, policemen, and railroad workers. Some Irish in the building trades became important contractors and suppliers of building materials. Women of Irish stock in 1900 were ser-

Mary Molloy, Dressmaker

In Minnesota, as in the East, many Irish women found work as dressmakers, seamstresses, and milliners. One who had considerable success was Mary O'Keefe Molloy. Her parents, Irish immigrants, arrived in St. Paul in the 1850s; her father, at first a day laborer, had found a good city job at the waterworks by 1885.

Mary was born in St. Paul in 1862 and evidently was apprenticed to Madame Adeline Paquette, a Paris-born dressmaker, in the 1870s. By 1879 Mary had her own dressmaking shop; in 1887 she married Herbert Molloy, a "refrigerator builder." Her business thrived. In the 1890s she employed more than 20 seamstresses and traveled to Paris every year to keep up with the latest fashions. Her clients included the state's wealthiest and most prominent women, who appreciated the fine fabrics, elaborate detail, exquisite workmanship, and elegant designs of her creations.

Employees in Mary Molloy's dressmaking shop, 1890

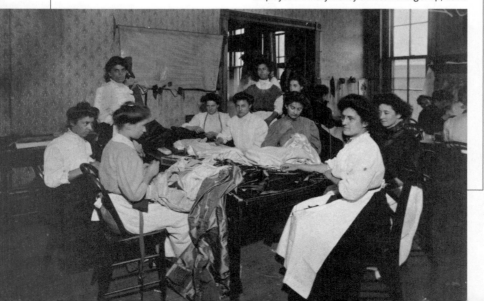

vants and waitresses (26%), dressmakers, seamstresses, and milliners (19%), and office workers (bookkeepers, clerks, copyists, stenographers, and "typewriters"—15%).[44]

As they did in the cities of the East, the Irish in St. Paul gravitated to the security and status of civil service jobs. In 1880 Irish immigrants made up a tenth of the city's working population, but they held 16% of the government jobs; two-fifths of the foreign born in these positions were Irish. The figures were virtually the same ten years later, when the Irish born constituted only 6% of the working population. By 1900, however, they began to share the category with the Germans.

Of these occupations the one that brought St. Paul's Irish special visibility was the police force. In 1858, 6 of the 11 police officers were Irish, and the Germans complained, asking for more representation. By 1878, 9 of 27 officers were Irish born. For the next 20 years about one-fourth of the policemen, firemen, and watchmen were Irish.[45]

St. Paul police officers and wagon in front of police headquarters, 1892–95

Part of a policeman's job at that time was to control vice by supervising it, a system common in the United States and used by St. Paul's Yankee mayors before 1884. That year marked the election of the city's second Irish-born mayor, Christopher D. O'Brien, who was an exception to the rule. O'Brien, the son of Dillon O'Brien, resolved to enforce the laws he had sworn to uphold—to the dismay of those most concerned. A history of the police and fire departments written in 1899 called his term "an epoch in municipal history," noting candidly that he proved "a great city can flourish apart from periodical fees paid it for tolerance of vice in its midst.... His term of office will always be remembered as the only 'closed administration' in the history of St. Paul." The police department's 1904 souvenir book commented that O'Brien "suppressed vice wherever he found it, with the result that it was continually cropping up in unexpected places."[46]

O'Brien and two of his brothers were lawyers, examples of a traditional Irish type. Trained in the English-controlled courts of Ireland, the Irish (stereotyped as silver tongued and quick witted) learned from the British how to manipulate the legal system. Irish-born lawyers in Minnesota and St. Paul were few in absolute numbers, but they formed a disproportionately large share of the foreign-born attorneys.[47]

Irish civil servants and lawyers were both a cause and an effect of the group's growing political power, and it is here that the city's social and economic structure supported the Irish. Historian Mary Wingerd provides a convincing analysis. In the 1850s and 1860s, wealthy St. Paulites had invested in the kinds of infrastructure and speculative activities available to those who arrived early on the frontier: banking, insurance, transportation, land along railroad corridors, timber. These businesses did not require control of a large local workforce. But in Minneapolis, where businessmen owned sawmills and flour mills, powerful capitalists needed tractable laborers, and they organized ruthlessly to get them. Furthermore, after the crash of 1858, St. Paul's business community, starved for capital, welcomed Irish and German small merchants. This meant that the city was relatively open to unions, relatively accepting of immigrant businesses, and relatively friendly to the laboring Irish and their political leaders.[48]

Because rural Minnesota was heavily Republican—between 1860 and 1955, only two Democrats were elected governor—control of St. Paul's Irish and German Democratic voters meant control of the state's small and isolated Democratic Party. The first politician to harness the voting power of the Irish was William Pitt Murray, a Scots Irish lawyer. In alliance with Louis Robert, who controlled the French vote, Murray directed the city's Democratic politics, holding various municipal and state offices from the 1850s until 1889. In the mid-1880s the leaders of the state Democratic Party were Patrick H. Kelly, a wholesale grocer, and Michael Doran, a banker and merchant, who allied themselves with railroad magnate James J. Hill. Both were Bourbon Democrats, well-to-do men who kept agrarian radicals out of power as they dispensed patronage after President Grover Cleveland's election in 1884.[49]

Hill, a Scots Irish Canadian and the richest, most powerful man in town, was Kelly's and Doran's silent partner, and Hill's participation was essential. He had married Mary Mehegan, a devout Irish Catholic who had attended school with John Ireland's sisters. Through Hill, the city's most

Archbishop John Ireland, Mary Mehegan Hill, and former governor Alexander Ramsey, 1902

exclusive social circles were open to Catholics; he showed a distinct preference for hiring Irish managers and contracting with Irish construction companies. Wingerd points out that Irish politicians and labor leaders used this entrée to become power brokers, establishing intraethnic alliances that balanced competing interests—and, as they had in larger eastern cities, they placed themselves at the fulcrum. St. Paul's working people, seeing that the city's economy rested on the success of the railroad, defended the industry against attacks from Republican farmers across the state and Republican businessmen in Minneapolis. Hill set higher rates for businesses in Minneapolis than in St. Paul, thus uniting St. Paul businessmen in opposition to reforms that might regulate rates.[50]

A St. Paul Writer

F. Scott Fitzgerald, who would become one of the greatest of American novelists and short story writers, benefited from St. Paul's social acceptance of the Irish. His mother's father, an Irish immigrant and a successful businessman, had married the daughter of an Irish immigrant carpenter. Fitzgerald once wrote to a friend: "I am half black Irish and half old American stock with the usual exaggerated ancestral pretensions. The black Irish half of the family had the money and looked down upon the Maryland side of the family. . . . So being born in that atmosphere of crack, wisecrack and countercrack I developed a two cylinder inferiority complex. . . . I spent my youth in alternately crawling in front of the kitchen maids and insulting the great."

Scottie and his mother, Molly McQuillan Fitzgerald, on Laurel Avenue in St. Paul, 1898

Shiely Construction Company cement truck, 1947. Shiely and other prominent construction firms owned by Irishmen were first hired by James J. Hill's Great Northern and later received large contracts from the archdiocese.

The Catholic church, with parishes in every ward and a hierarchy controlled by Archbishop John Ireland, was a participant. Ireland may have been a prominent Republican, but he was also a booster for St. Paul and a business associate of Hill's. Because John Ireland favored Irish clergy, and Irish clergy assisted Irish parishioners, the fortunes of the church, the Irish, and the city were interdependent. To build new churches, the St. Paul Seminary, and the Colleges of St. Thomas and St. Catherine, Ireland hired construction firms owned by Irishmen—Foley Brothers, Butler Brothers, and Shiely Sand and Gravel, for example, all of whom got their start building Hill's Great Northern line—and they in turn hired skilled Irish workers.[51]

In 1889, when the older leaders bungled an election by nominating a city ticket top-heavy with Irishmen, new Irish politicians took over direction of the party. Richard T. and John J. O'Connor were sons of a boardinghouse operator and local politician. Richard, who clerked for Hill's Minneapolis, Manitoba, and Pacific Railroad as a young man, became deputy city clerk in 1880 and served

Richard T. ("The Cardinal") O'Connor was so nicknamed because he had power greater than that of Archbishop John Ireland, who never became one. His brother John J. ("The Big Fellow") was the creator of the O'Connor system.

his political internship under the Irish leadership in city hall. In alliance with William Hamm, Sr., a German brewer, he rebuilt the party. Like Kelly and Doran, O'Connor was closely associated with Hill, and he became one of the most influential Democrats in the country after 1904. His brother John had worked in Patrick Kelly's grocery house before joining the police force in 1881. He became police chief in 1901 and held the position for 19 years.[52]

The brothers were the originators of the "O'Connor system," a scheme whereby criminals across the country were told that they would not be arrested in St. Paul as long as they obeyed the law while within the city. The O'Connors oversaw the heyday of prostitution, including the operations of Nina Clifford, a famous madam of Irish Canadian heritage whose house was around the corner from the police station. Many of their gangster contacts were Irish, as well; "Dapper Dan" Hogan was St. Paul's fixer. St. Paul citizens knew and approved of these arrangements, which brought security to their streets. But the O'Connors left St. Paul politics (James retired in 1920 and Richard became more involved in national politics) just as St. Paul became a leading bootlegging town, and violent gangsters soon followed. In 1932 more than a fifth of the country's bank robberies took place in Minnesota, carried out by the Dillinger and Barker-Karpis gangs. The system finally began to break down when William Hamm, Jr., and Edward Bremer, another prominent St. Paul brewer, were kidnapped in 1933 and 1934, respectively. Powerful St. Paulites, fearing they might be the next victims, called in help from Washington.[53]

The O'Connor system epitomizes the insularity that Wingerd identifies as "the defining feature of culture in St. Paul." St. Paul's Irish were at the center of a system that delivered on the promises made to city residents; "though outsiders might derisively label St. Paul as an Irish-Catholic town, within its borders the labels 'Irish' and 'Catholic' were badges of no small community status." As the economy of Minneapolis boomed, St. Paul became a quiet, stable community, and that was what its residents wanted.[54]

More liberal Irish politicians opposed these conservative officials. Their best-known challenger was Ignatius Donnelly, politician, writer, and Populist philosopher who was born in Philadelphia in 1831 to an Irish immigrant father and a second-generation Irish mother. He moved in 1857 to Minnesota, where he entered territorial politics, helped found the townsite of Nininger on the Mississippi River in Dakota County, and wrote a number of literary, scientific, and political books of enduring, if unconventional, interest. During the next 43 years, Donnelly was associated with many parties—Democratic, Republican, Granger, Anti-Monopolist, Greenback, Farmers' Alliance, People's, and Populist—and he battled with the leaders of each. He was lieutenant governor when the Civil War

Ignatius Donnelly, 1898, and at home (seated at left, with child on his lap) with his family in Nininger, 1893

broke out and a representative in Congress from 1863 to 1869. Although he failed in five tries to regain a congressional seat, he became a favorite of Dakota County's Irish and Populist voters, who elected him to the state legislature six times. Donnelly was a talented, humorous, and popular speaker, a perennial favorite who addressed Irish gatherings and St. Patrick's Day functions to loud and prolonged cheers.[55]

Another opponent of the conservative Democrats and the man who introduced Donnelly to the most successful national Populist of his day, William Jennings Bryan, was James Manahan. An Irish lawyer born in Chatfield in 1866, Manahan made his reputation as a Populist by arguing various lawsuits to lower the railroads' shipping, Pullman, and express rates and to break the monopoly of the Minneapolis and Chicago grain exchanges. His reformist politics made him by turns a Bryan Democrat, a Progressive Republican, and a leader of the Nonpartisan League; he served one term in Congress, from 1913 to 1915.[56]

James Manahan, Populist Irish lawyer, 1890

Maintaining Community and Identity

Even as they pursued jobs and political power in the cities and around the state, Minnesota's Irish maintained ties with the homeland. Two major Irish newspapers served both aims. The *Northwestern Chronicle,* official paper of the Catholic archdiocese, was printed in St. Paul from 1866 to 1900. The *Irish Standard,* founded in 1885 in Minneapolis as the *Northwest Standard,* was a semiofficial and, from 1915 to its demise in 1920, official paper of the Ancient Order of Hibernians. Both carried Catholic, Irish, and Minnesota news, anti-British editorials, columns on Irish history and politics, agricultural reports, serialized fiction, and social items. They printed news, notes, and advertisements from Irish communities throughout the state and, to a lesser extent, the region.[57]

One of the earliest and most active of the many organizations to demonstrate an interest in the homeland was the Fenian Brotherhood, which was organized in New York in the 1850s to give political, financial, and military aid to revolutionaries in Ireland. By the end of the Civil War, with thousands of Irish veterans returning to their homes in the northern United States, the organization split. One faction wanted to continue to support Irish revolutionaries. The other wanted to organize the Irish veterans and to attack the British crown more directly, by invading Canada. A representative of the latter faction spoke to a gathering of "some three or four hundred Irishmen and women" in St. Paul in March 1866, attempting to organize a local Fenian circle, but he made an error in nominating Father John Ireland to serve as the group's secretary. Ireland asked to speak and then argued eloquently against supporting an organization that was so divided. The stunned organizer was unable to respond, and the meeting collapsed.[58]

Two months later, Fenians in New York attempted an unsuccessful invasion of Canada; soon afterward, Fenian circles were formed in Minnesota, Wisconsin, and Iowa. The groups' activities aroused speculation in local newspapers, especially with regard to gunrunning. In 1870, after the pope decreed that Fenian members were subject to excommunication and a second invasion of Canada failed, the group's influence waned. But St. Paul's former Fenians, reorganized as the United Irishmen, helped launch an attack on Canada in 1871. The plans were laid in St. Paul with the ardent support of Minnesotans who hoped to make Manitoba part of the United States. Led by ex-Fenians General John O'Neill and William B. O'Donoghue, a force of about 35 made for Canada, where they hoped to unite with Louis Riel's Métis people and march on Winnipeg to strike a blow against the British. On October 5 they captured the Hudson's Bay Company post just north of the international border at Pembina, North Dakota, before being taken prisoner by U.S. soldiers.[59]

Irish patriotic groups formed in subsequent years proposed to work more peacefully for the political freedom and economic improvement of Ireland. For example, the constitution of the Friends of Ireland, organized in St. Paul in August 1877, stated: "We hold that Ireland belongs to the Irish people, in Ireland; that they are the nation; that it is for them to select their form of government; for them to speak, to act; for us, their friends, to assist."[60]

Direct assistance was forthcoming in the late 1870s, when yet another famine struck Ireland. Chapters of the Irish National Land League were formed to help dispossessed farmers buy back their land. Charles Stewart Parnell, the Irish Protestant founder of the movement, traveled throughout the United States soliciting funds. He visited Minnesota in February 1880, speaking to wildly enthusiastic crowds in Winona, Lake City, St. Paul, and Minneapolis. In St. Paul, Coadjutor Bishop Ireland and a group of politicians received Parnell, who remarked that he thought land reform, rather than emigration, was the solution to his homeland's problems. The bishop asked nonetheless for Parnell's support of the Catholic Colonization Bureau. "A word from you will do a thousand times more than pamphlets or articles on the subject," said Ireland. The Land Leaguer's speech in St. Paul raised $1,700; he addressed a similar rally in Minneapolis later that evening. Irish from other parts of the state also contributed hundreds of dollars in the following weeks and months.[61]

Many of the Irish organizations that joined in these relief efforts were oriented primarily toward social life in the Twin Cities. Among them were drill teams (such as the Wolfe Tone Rifles of Minneapolis and the Emmet Light

Artillery of St. Paul), literary societies, and social clubs. Irish drama, music, and comedy were presented in the 1870s in performances called Hibernicons, and festivals were held honoring such famous Irishmen as Robert Emmet and Thomas Moore.[62]

More prominent and longer lived was the Ancient Order of Hibernians (AOH), organized in the state in 1879, and its women's auxiliary, formed in 1894. Both groups functioned as mutual benefit societies and as organizers of such Irish celebrations as St. Patrick's Day. By 1912 there were 82 AOH divisions in the state. The Ladies' Auxiliary, which had organized 68 divisions by 1949, also raised funds for civic and Catholic projects.[63]

A great number of the organizations that donated to Irish relief were chapters of temperance or total-abstinence societies. The Catholic church led the way in this effort, beginning as early as 1852, when Bishop Cretin organized the Catholic Temperance Society of St. Paul. The movement did not take hold, however, until after the Civil War. Then

The Ladies' Auxiliary of the Ancient Order of Hibernians, Kilkenny, about 1910

the Father Mathew Temperance Society, organized in 1868 at Belle Plaine, enrolled 170 members in less than a month. The movement received greater impetus in January 1869. As John Ireland told the story, a group of Irish drinkers in a St. Paul saloon, deciding to reform, signed a petition that read, "For God's sake organize a Temperance Society." An apparently inebriated member of the group set off to deliver the petition to Ireland, who immediately agreed to the request.[64]

From these humble beginnings the movement grew rapidly. The Father Mathew Temperance Society of Cathedral parish set an example that was touted far and wide by the *Northwestern Chronicle* and the considerable energies of John Ireland. The greatest boom in membership occurred in 1875, when Paulist missionaries lectured throughout the diocese, gaining hundreds of recruits. In that year, too, Ireland became a bishop, a position that gave him a wider platform from which to urge the cause. By 1882 there were 62 branches throughout the state.[65]

Early temperance efforts emphasized setting up branches and recruiting members. Because many who took the pledge did not keep it, the societies worked to retain members, most of whom were working-class Irish. In the early 1870s they sponsored social functions and, in some cases, offered libraries, marching bands, and glee clubs to replace the pleasures of the saloons. Such societies marched in St. Patrick's Day parades and at church celebrations. Some provided mutual assistance. After 1873 many parishes started Cadet or Crusader groups for young men, in order to reduce the friction that developed among members of different ages. A statewide temperance union formed in 1872 held annual conventions. Women's groups were belatedly initiated in 1876.[66]

Although these groups were called temperance societies, they really advocated total abstinence, and in early years their members were fined or expelled for imbibing.

But total abstinence was a difficult challenge for many and, in a city known for large breweries, a political issue. While Ireland led a successful campaign in 1886 to raise drastically the cost of liquor licenses in Minnesota, thereby reducing the number of taverns, he later carefully adjusted the pledge of the Crusader's Total Abstinence Society, allowing both moderate drinkers and total abstainers to belong.[67]

It is difficult to judge the success of temperance organizations in reforming chronic drinkers. Church accounts are uniformly laudatory. The *St. Paul Pioneer Press,* perhaps a less biased observer, commented in 1882: "It was not many years ago that the Catholic Irish of St. Paul contributed a large proportion of the drunken, disorderly, and rowdy elements of the community. . . . From the most intemperate, disorderly, and unthrifty, they have, as a rule, become among the most temperate, orderly, industrious, thrifty and moral classes of the community." The transformation was credited to John Ireland's temperance work.[68]

Ireland's influence on Catholics of other nationalities was often equally dramatic. He and other church leaders, most of them Irish, wanted to produce a distinctly Ameri-

Jack Gibbons and Fred Lenhart at the St. Paul Auditorium on April 17, 1936. At the time Lenhart was one of only two fighters ever to beat Gibbons in a professional match.

can Catholic church that would be acceptable to the country's Protestant majority. In attempting to show critics that Catholics were patriotic Americans whose duties and devotion to the state matched those of other groups, Ireland assumed the task of mediating between old-stock Americans and new immigrants. But for many European Catholics, the church was the center of community social life. When the archbishop closed the beer gardens and bazaars and began to discourage the use of native languages, he was threatening the religious as well as the ethnic identity of communities already struggling for survival in an alien land. He was accused of imposing Irish Catholicism, and he met bitter resistance.[69]

A more acceptable form of the Hibernicization of Minnesotans began to operate in the early 1850s. St. Patrick's Day assumed a special role in Minnesota as the beginning of the end of the long winter. The *Minnesota Democrat* of March 17, 1852, announced that the day would be celebrated with a procession and a supper, "a pleasant and joyous gathering of the warm hearted sons of Erin, *and their countrymen of all nations*" (emphasis in original). Two years

Irish Boxers

Boxing, which requires no fancy equipment and no expensive club fees, has long been the sport of immigrants and the underprivileged. Minnesota's Irishmen were boxing fanatics, and they had some great homegrown boxers to cheer. Patsy Cardiff, fighting the great John L. Sullivan in 1887, broke a bone in his opponent's arm; the fight ended in a draw in the sixth round. Mike O'Dowd was the middleweight champion of the world before and after serving overseas in World War I. In 1923, Tommy Gibbons, ducking and weaving, went 15 rounds with Jack Dempsey in the famous heavyweight prize fight at Shelby, Montana, finally losing the decision. (Gibbons, whose brother Mike and nephew Jack were also prominent boxers, later served as Ramsey County sheriff for 20 years.) Jim Beattie, six feet seven inches tall, played The Kid in the movie *The Great White Hope*.

Newspaper columnist Nick Coleman, recalling his boyhood in St. Paul in the 1950s, remembered that boxing was "a St. Paul obsession. . . . Every old man I knew had once been a boxer. My Grandpa Coleman even boxed his own brother on one occasion, so the promoters changed his name to Spiderlegs Jackson."

later the festivities included some 18 toasts in honor of various dignitaries and institutions: elected officials of the United States and Minnesota, the press, the legal profession, women, and England's enemy in the Crimean War, "The Russian Bear; So fond of Honey, may she soon get her fill of Turkey." The group also drank to their fellow immigrants and guests, "the Natives of Foreign Countries; Naturalized citizens of the United States now celebrating the day with Us."[70]

Festivities became more elaborate in the 1860s, setting a pattern followed for many years. The day began with a High Mass at the Cathedral, which usually included a sermon mourning the oppression of Ireland, praising the faith of the Irish, and extolling the virtues of temperance. After the service, such organizations as the temperance society and the Knights of St. Paul paraded with lavish green-silk and gold-braided banners, marching behind the Great Western Band to the bishop's house, where they heard a second address. For many years the speaker was John Ireland, who used the occasion to arouse pride and anger in his audience and to channel those emotions into resolutions for self-improvement. Sometimes the marchers stopped at the Sisters of St. Joseph convent and orphanage to pay their respects and play music for the children. The procession would then call upon the governor or the mayor for speeches as well.[71]

After that the participants adjourned until evening, when various entertainments were scheduled. In the early years one hall held all, but later several parishes sponsored separate observances. The programs featured sketches, music, dances, and recitations. A typical event at Mozart Hall in 1869 included the tableaux "The Emigrant Boy Leaving His Father's Cot," "Erin," and "Emmet's Trial"; for musical entertainment, lyrically announced the *Northwestern Chronicle*, "One of our amateurs will sing 'Soggarth Aroon' [Beloved Priest], 'Kathleen Mavourneen,' and after having melted us to tears by the suavity of those lyrics, will set us in high glee by his rendering of 'The Irish Schoolmaster.'"[72]

So many non-Irish turned out in 1860 that the *Pioneer and Democrat,* a Republican paper, was moved to complain. Such celebrations, it said, "should be made more truly representative of the nation participating in them, by addresses from their own speakers, their national and characteristic music, &c., especially where, as in this instance, the requisite talent can be found, without going out of their own ranks." But the practice was continued and expanded. The St. Patrick's Day celebration at St. Vincent's parish in 1909 included a performance by Charles Young, a Chinese American Catholic, who sang "Killarney" and "Come Back to Erin" in Chinese to "thunderous applause."[73]

These celebrations were occasions for much visiting among Minnesota's Irish communities. Seven hundred Irishmen gathered in Rochester in 1867 for speeches, supper, song, and the viewing of "eight pyramidal cakes, from three to four feet high." In 1875 seven temperance societies from Goodhue and Wabasha Counties met at Lake City to mark the day. The AOH arranged special railroad rates for those who wished to travel to St. Paul for the festivities in 1901, when 4,000 men marched in the parade. The occasion could also renew contact with Ireland, as it did for Winonans who received shamrocks from the Old Country to wear on St. Patrick's Day in 1909.[74]

The parade in 1901 was the last in St. Paul for 66 years. Local tradition has it that Archbishop Ireland, objecting to rowdy behavior of participants, stopped the parades. Observances continued in church halls, and the AOH and its auxiliary sponsored open houses, dances, and dinners throughout the next several decades. Many of these were held at the Hibernian Hall on West 7th Street.[75]

World War I challenged Irish communities across the United States, including those in Minnesota. Before the

Sons of an Irish immigrant, labor leaders Vincent Raymond, Miles, and Grant Dunne, with William Brown, organized the striking truck drivers of Teamsters Local 574 in the Truck Strike of 1934, which ended the period of the closed shop in Minneapolis. Briefly imprisoned by Governor Floyd B. Olson, Vince and Miles Dunne and Brown were released on August 2 from the military stockade at the state fairgrounds. Left to right: Grant Dunne, William Brown, Miles Dunne, Vince Dunne, and attorney Albert Goldman.

United States went to war, the *Irish Standard* printed articles defending Germany's claims against Britain; during the war, its pages were full of patriotic stories. Although many Americans opposed the conflict as a rich man's war, fought by the poor, there was no organized protest by St. Paul's Irish community. Wingerd suggests that the Irish, who were both rich and poor, could not afford to argue the matter. Both could see the advantages of retaining a unified voice in the city. There were, however, some activities in support of an Irish republic. Various groups passed resolutions and sponsored lectures by Irish politicians; some people bought bonds in the new Free State in the 1920s. By the 1930s, activity in Minnesota relating to homeland politics had died down.[76]

The Other Sullivans

The five Sullivan brothers from Minneapolis who fought in World War II all returned home safely and watched in 1946 as their mother, Sarah Donnelly Sullivan, an Irish immigrant, removed the Service Stars from her window. The act was all the more poignant for the family's thoughts of the five brothers from Waterloo, Iowa, also named Sullivan, who were killed when their ship was sunk in battle off Guadalcanal in 1942. The Minnesota brothers all married; their children grew up hearing of the Iowa Sullivans and watching *The Fighting Sullivans,* the patriotic movie made in 1944 as part of the war effort. "I always got from my dad," remembered Don's daughter Patty Sullivan, "that you should live life to the fullest. He'd say, 'There's this family in Iowa . . .'"

Jim, Bill, Art, Don, Ed, and Sarah Sullivan

Irish participation in Minnesota Democratic politics did not slow, however. In 1920, when 11 of the 12 members of the State Democratic Executive Committee were Irish, the *St. Paul Pioneer Press* commented that there were "enough Irishmen in the list to make up a creditable ball team" and suggested that the single non-Irishman should be the umpire. Between 1932 and 1972, all but one of the 10 men who served as mayors of St. Paul—some of them Republicans—had Irish surnames.[77]

The control these conservative Democrats had over the party was responsible for its weakness in the state. Apparently forgetting the earlier examples of William Pitt Murray and Richard T. O'Connor, they ran heavily Irish tickets that historian Millard Gieske called "appropriate for Boston politics." The party was split, with Irish Americans on both sides. But in 1940 a coalition of labor, more moderate Farmer-Laborites, and Catholic Democrats, backing John J. McDonough for mayor, won an impressive victory that foreshadowed the parties' merger four years later. St. Paul Irish politicians figured prominently in the formation of the Democratic-Farmer-Labor Party in 1944.[78]

In the mid-1940s, at war's end, there was an economic downturn in Ireland and a renewal of emigration. The Twin City Irish-American Club, formed by some of the younger immigrants who had arrived at the beginning of the Great Depression, held weekly dances and offered assistance to the newcomers, including help finding work. In the early 1950s, an Irishman with good connections downtown could get a city job for an immigrant friend. As late as 1957, a political study judged that being Catholic was "almost essential for political success in St. Paul" and that the Irish were the predominant Catholic group. This trend slowed, however, as affirmative action and civil service legislation diminished patronage hiring, and the Irish became less prominent in city politics.[79]

Being American, Remembering Roots

By the early 1900s, the great mass of Irish immigration to the United States had ended, although Irish men and women continued to cross the ocean to join family members. The numbers followed economic and political conditions: there was little immigration during the world wars and the depression, and also during the 1960s, when Ireland's economy boomed and the threat of the American draft kept males, especially, from making the trip. The immigrants of the 1800s aged and died; their children and grandchildren took the opportunities offered by the new land and became successful, achieving higher educational and income levels than immigrants from other European countries. Ethnic pride was not much celebrated in the 1950s, although the election of President John F. Kennedy in 1960 brought a new measure of pride and acceptance to Irish Americans. By the 1970s a new interest in Irish culture was showing itself across the country. And the publication in 1976 of Alex Haley's *Roots* inspired Americans of all ethnicities to learn more about their families and their heritage.[80]

Minnesota's Irish participated in all these trends. In part, this reflected the group's urbanization. In 1900, 40% of Minnesota's workers made their living on the land; by the end of the century, less than 4% did so, and Irish American farmers were among those who moved to town. Beginning with the postwar building boom of the 1950s, growing suburbs encroached on farmlands close to the

From Irish Farm to Suburb

As St. Paul and Minneapolis have grown, they have encroached on farms still held by descendants of early Irish settlers. The community of Cahill, settled in 1854 in the southern part of what is now Edina, offers an excellent example. Well past 1900, while the New Englanders to the north built businesses, market gardens, and ties to Minneapolis, the conservative Irish farmers in the south preferred to maintain a thoroughly rural community. The town maintained two school districts, carefully gerrymandered to keep Catholic and Protestant children in different schools. Electricity finally came to Cahill in the 1930s. But in the postwar housing boom of the 1950s, the farms of the Irish were swallowed by suburban housing and commercial developments, including the Southdale shopping center. "A few of us are a little irked when people talk about the 'cake eaters' of Edina," complained a farmer whose family had been in the area since 1854. "We farmers go way back, and there was no cake laying around here when we grew up."

The farm of John Tierney, a descendant of one of Cahill's founding families, at the Edina-Richfield-Minneapolis border near West 60th Street, 1954

Twin Cities, forcing descendants of the earliest Irish farming families in Dakota and Hennepin Counties to sell. Tracking those who remained is difficult. In 1976 the Minnesota Agricultural Society began to list farms that had been held by the same family for 100 years. Descendants of Irish-born farmers owned 11% of the "century farms" in the eight counties that had the largest Irish populations in 1870—counties where the Irish born had made up just 7% of the 1870 populations. In 1990 the U.S. census, which carried out a statistical sampling of ancestry, estimated that 10% of all Minnesotans living in places with populations under 2,500 claimed some Irish heritage, as did 8% of the people who were actually farming. Several communities in the middle of these farming areas supported long-running St. Patrick's Day parades: New Ulm (since 1966), St. Peter (1979), Belle Plaine (1972), Le Center (1984), and Waseca (1969).[81]

These celebrations were organized by Irish Americans, but they all demonstrate a familiar good-natured ethnic inclusiveness that reached remarkable proportions in Duluth, where relatively few Irish and Irish Americans were actually involved. In the 1970s, when interest in folk dancing brought some ceilis (traditional Irish dances) to the city, the sponsors were a political interest group, a neighborhood association, and food cooperatives. The semiannual dances, held for the first few years in the Sons of Norway Hall, drew many Finnish American participants. When a St. Patrick's Day parade was revived in 1971, one of the founders was Jewish, and the participants included the Italian-American Club. By 2001, Sir Benedict's Tavern on the Lake, an English-themed bar, sponsored a popular weekly Celtic jam session. But a joke among Iron Rangers in the 1950s, featuring a fictional Finnish saint who drove the grasshoppers from the vineyards of Finland, blossomed into a holiday that was more celebrated than that of the Irish. St. Urho's Day is enthusiastically observed on

Minnesota's Irish Americans continued to participate in state politics. In 1964 Senator Eugene McCarthy, who was born in Watkins, Minnesota, rode in a parade with his daughters Ellen, Mary, and Margaret; in 1968, vehemently opposing U.S. involvement in the Vietnam War, he ran for the presidency. McCarthy's protégé, Nicholas Coleman, became majority leader of Minnesota's state senate. That body's self-described "Irish Caucus"—State Senators Emily Anne Staples, Coleman, and Edward J. Gearty—cut a shamrock cake on St. Patrick's Day 1978, Gearty's birthday.

March 16 by purple-clad Finns in Duluth, on the iron ranges, and in Finnish communities across the country.[82]

Immigration decreased when the Irish economy boomed in the 1960s and early 1970s, but it rose again from the late 1970s to the late 1990s, when the country's economy slowed again. As Ireland's unemployment rate hit 20%, young, educated Irish men and women emigrated, many taking illegal jobs in New York, Boston, and San Francisco as nannies and restaurant and construction workers. In the Twin Cities, where the community is much smaller, that does not seem to have been the case.[83]

In 1990 about 430,000 residents of the Twin Cities metropolitan area, or 15% of the total, claimed Irish ancestry. The percentage was the same in the central cities, where heaviest concentrations lived in highly desirable neighborhoods: the western part of St. Paul and the southwestern parts of Minneapolis, near the lakes. An astonishing wealth of organized groups in the Twin Cities Irish community reflected the diverse political, social, and cultural interests of Irish Americans.[84]

Political activists, spurred by the renewed troubles in Ireland, found various ways to participate. Minnesota Irish Northern Aid, established in 1974, sends money to the dependents of Catholic political prisoners in Northern Ireland. A Minnesota chapter of the Irish American Unity Conference coordinates the efforts of American groups working to bring peace to Ireland. Minnesotans for a United Ireland, a successor to the H Block/Armagh Committee, sponsors cultural and political events to educate Americans about what the group sees as British oppression in Northern Ireland; for some years members commemorated the Easter Uprising at the grave of Fenian William B. O'Donoghue in Rosemount. The Children's Program of Northern Ireland started in 1972, when a Brainerd family offered a summer home to a Belfast boy

The MacBride Principles

In 1987 six of Minnesota's Irish groups—the Ancient Order of Hibernians, the Ladies' AOH, the American Irish Political Education Committee, Minnesotans for a United Ireland, the Twin Cities Irish American Club, and Minnesota Irish Northern Aid—formed a chapter of the Irish American Unity Conference and began to urge support for the McBride Principles, a set of employment guidelines designed to counter discrimination against Catholics in Northern Ireland. Companies doing business in Northern Ireland were asked to adopt the principles; the British government strongly opposed the campaign, arguing that the controversy would discourage the foreign investment needed for the area's economic development. Minnesota's Irish Americans lobbied the state legislature to mandate that state pension funds be invested only in companies that adopted the principles. Early in March of 1988 St. Paul's city council passed such a mandate, making it the first city in Minnesota to do so. A month later, in spite of heavy lobbying by the British consulate in Chicago, the legislature followed suit, and Minnesota became the first state outside the Northeast to pass legislation in support of the principles.

At the signing of the bill supporting the principles, April 1988: John Curtin, Leah Curtin, Thomond O'Brien, Kathy Foley, Governor Rudy Perpich, Jerry Hughes, Margaret Kelly, and Bill Gleason

whose mother wanted him to have a temporary escape from the violence of his community. The Hibbing Rotary Club took up the cause, and the program has expanded to regular six-week summer trips for about 125 10- and 11-year-old children from Northern Ireland, half Protestant and half Catholic, who stay with families in the Twin Cities and around the state. The program enjoys widespread support, including an annual fund-raising soccer match between teams sponsored by Kieran's Irish Pub and Brit's Pub in Minneapolis.[85]

Other groups focused less on politics and more on culture. The men's and women's Hibernian organizations had fewer than 300 members at the end of the century. Leaders of the state organizations provided essential direction and support for many other political and cultural activities. By the mid-1990s the Hibernian Life Insurance Fund of Minnesota was the last of its kind in the country. It offered scholarships for members' children and organized the Irish program for the St. Paul Festival of Nations. The Irish Genealogical Society, International, with 2,300 members from across the United States and other countries, is the largest of its kind in the United States. Gaeltacht Minnesota has taught weekly language classes in Irish since 1981. In the 1980s the Twin City Irish-American Club became inactive, but Failte Minnesota was organized in 2001 to take its place. Irish Books and Media, founded in 1970, became the largest wholesaler of Irish books and cultural materials in the United States. The *Irish Gazette,* published since 1984, carries local and international news items, notices of upcoming events, and advertisements aimed at the community, including those placed by a dozen Irish pubs in the metro area that serve as gathering places and venues for music. Law enforcement officers of Irish descent established the Emerald Society of Minnesota in 1992. Na Fianna Irish Players, a community theater formed in 1988 by Irish and Irish Americans, produces two plays a year.[86]

The largest Irish cultural organization in the United States, the Irish American Cultural Institute, was started in Minnesota in 1962 by Eoin McKiernan, a second-generation Irishman from upstate New York. Reasoning that an organization in the Midwest might escape the factional politics of the Irish in the East, he found strong support among St. Paul's Irish and at the College of St. Thomas. When the IACI was moved to New Jersey in 1995, St. Thomas promptly established a Center for Irish Studies, which fosters study about Ireland; publishes the *New Hibernia Review,* the only quarterly journal of Irish studies in North America; and presents the annual Lawrence O'Shaughnessy Award for Poetry.[87]

A revival of Irish music and dance that began in St. Paul in the mid-1970s grew into a thriving cultural scene in the following decades, supported by those with a New Age interest in Celtic customs. The Irish Music and Dance Association of Minnesota, active since 1977, sponsored

Bob Sweeney dancing to music provided by John McCormick behind MacCafferty's Pub on Grand Avenue in St. Paul, 1981

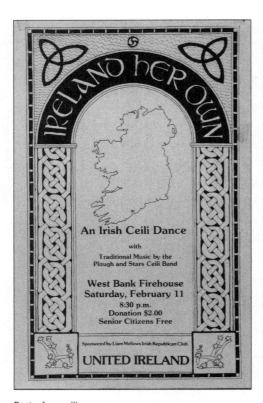

Poster for a ceili in Minneapolis, 1978

appearances of touring Irish musicians and dancers. Several organizations organized regular ceilis in the 1970s and 1980s, providing dance instruction to newcomers. Observers agree that the success of Riverdance, the Irish music and dance spectacle first performed in 1994, boosted interest in dance lessons by Irish Americans and many others. By 2001 there were three Irish step-dance studios and four performance groups in the state. The Brian Boru Pipe Band, established in 1961, and the Minnesota Pipes and Drums, organized by the Emerald Society in the mid-1990s, performed at festivals and at funerals of law enforcement officers. And Irish musicians of international fame, including Paddy O'Brien, Seán O'Driscoll, and Daithi Sproule, have made their homes in the Twin Cities, attracted by the supportive and nonpoliticized community.[88]

In 1980, frustrated by what they saw as the perversion of Irish culture and celebration of drunkenness that had come to characterize St. Patrick's Day in St. Paul, a group of Irish Americans connected with the Hibernians started an annual Irish celebration, which is held in the late summer or fall. In 2001 the two-day Irish Fair of Minnesota drew about 25,000 people from the Twin Cities and across the state. Archbishop Harry Flynn celebrated a Catholic Mass on Sunday morning; participants enjoyed a dozen Irish musical groups performing on two stages, eight dance troupes, more than 50 vendors selling Irish materials and

At a St. Paul Irish Fair in the 1990s, small children danced to Irish music; Linne Rund and Thomond O'Brien tended a booth.

providing information on causes, and tents with children's activities, storytelling, and plays. Food vendors reflected both the Irish and the Minnesotan, selling lamb stew and corn dogs, soda bread and deep-fried cheese curds.[89]

Observances of St. Patrick's Day in St. Paul at the beginning of the 21st century followed familiar patterns. The day began with a special St. Patrick's Day Mass, celebrated by the archbishop, that filled the Cathedral of St. Paul. Among those attending were delegations from the city's police and firefighting forces, as well as the Hibernians, both men and women, who marched in full regalia. The St. Patrick's Day parade, revived in 1967, consisted mostly of community and family groups carrying identifying banners, some from southeastern Minnesota Irish settlements. A green stripe painted down 5th Street marked the route, which was lined by tens of thousands of onlookers. Green clothing was the fashion of the day; green faces, hair, and dogs were not uncommon; an Irish Elvis wore a sequined cape with a huge shamrock and spoke with a brogue ("Top o' the marnin' to yuh, mama"). After the parade, the crowds split. Many revelers flocked to downtown bars. Others headed for Landmark Center, where since 1991 there have been programs of Irish music and dance, lectures, and booths offering Irish imports and political information.[90]

Organizers of this essentially civic function carry on the tradition of inviting non-Irish to join, and the non-

Green hats, flags, and plastic horns at the St. Paul parade in 1978

Since the 1850s, St. Paul's celebration of St. Patrick's Day has welcomed groups representing other nationalities. The 1970 parade included the Ballet Folklórico Guadalupano, a dance group based at Our Lady of Guadalupe Church on St. Paul's West Side.

Irish oblige. The day is a springtime bacchanal, a northern Mardi Gras, with the boastful Irish generously providing an excuse for other Minnesotans to celebrate the winter's end and spend money in downtown St. Paul. Many of St. Paul's Irish scrupulously avoid the revelry, disliking the identification of Irishness with drunkenness and of Irish culture with green paint, shamrocks, and shillelaghs. Others take a more casual view, enjoying the opportunity to identify with their heritage and feeling comfortable enough with the success of the Irish to laugh at the stereotypes.

These differences in reactions, like those to Governor Ventura's joke, reflect the variety of attitudes about Irishness and the many ways Americans see themselves. The old set of stereotypes can be paired with a matching set of new ones: the immigrants lived in ethnic communities, where they belonged to mutual aid societies, listened to the music of their childhoods, dreamed of visiting their families in the Old Country, and strove to become American; the descendants live in the suburbs, where they may decide to join Irish organizations, buy Irish sweaters and compact discs, dream of traveling to Ireland to find relatives, and, within their thoroughly American identities, strive to find ways to be Irish. For many descendants of northern Europeans, ethnic identity and its markers has become a matter of individual choice.[91] And the Minnesotans who attend Irish-themed events—old families from Minnesota communities marching proudly together, new immigrants, college students enjoying a citywide party, lovers of Irish music and dance, baby boomers suddenly discovering their families' histories—all have their own reasons, all make their own choices, and all tell their own stories.

Personal Account:
A Domestic Worker's Journal

by Winnifred Lydon

In 1908, when Winnifred Therese Lydon was about 18, she immigrated from Cappaduff, County Mayo, to St. Paul, Minnesota. Her aunt Mary, who lived on the city's East Side, had sent her money for passage.

Lydon was one of more than 700,000 Irish women who left Ireland between 1885 and 1920 for opportunities in the United States. More women than men made the trip during those years, and almost 90% of the women between 15 and 35 were single. No other country saw this great a proportion of young women leave, but Irish conditions had continued to promote emigration. As market farming overtook subsistence farming, landholdings were consolidated, so women's labor was less needed and fewer men were able to marry. Thousands of women, like their brothers, realized that their best opportunity lay abroad.

Irish women found a niche in the U.S. labor market as domestic servants. Women of many other cultures were not permitted to work outside the home; Irish families had no such tradition, and in fact they often depended on wages contributed by daughters, whether working in Ireland or sending remittances from the United States. Winnifred Lydon soon joined their numbers. She first worked in a commercial laundry, which she hated for its noise, then found work with a family. In 1911 Kate Lydon, a woman who shared her last name and would soon marry her brother Mike, found Winnifred a job as a chambermaid in the spacious Summit Avenue home of Louis W. and Maude Taylor Hill. Winnifred earned $30 per month and spent parts of several summers at North Oaks, the hobby farm north of St. Paul owned by James J. Hill, Louis's father.

When Winnifred emigrated, she began keeping a journal, periodically writing down the events of the previous months or years. The document is fragmentary and tantalizing: she names people without identifying them, refers to stories that she does not tell, and uses dates intermittently. Her words show the fun of her life and her strong attachment to Ireland but little of her day-to-day work routine. In 1915 she left the Hills and married John Philben, a railroad laborer who had temporarily worked as a gardener at

John Philben and Winnifred Lydon Philben at their wedding, 1915. Standing are Winnifred's brother Michael Lydon and her cousin Anna Olsem.

Hill's house. The Philbens had three children. Winnifred died in St. Paul in 1972.

Left Cappaduff on Wednesday morning 29th April 1908 at 11:30 A.M. arrived at Queenstown at 10 P.M. wet & drowsy. Wrote & sent 8 postals. Up at 6 A.M. Thursday 30th April got ready for Tender to sail on Caronia but too foggy tried 3 times but all in vain. Sad & sore, sick & tired. Detained at Queenstown until Sunday 3rd May which was bright & clear. Got up at 5 A.M. & got ready for Tender to sail on Mauretania at 11 A.M. got on Board felt sickly but not too bad.... Arrived following Saturday in New York at noon. Took 6:30 train for St. Paul. Arrived in St. Paul Tuesday 8:15 A.M. 12th May 1908 met Aunt Mary & Uncle Michael Comiskey & Jim Collins at Depot. How glad I felt, how happy.

Spent a good time till May 19th Mike went to work to Hamline. I went to work in the factory 29th May 1908. (how I hated it)....

Wore my dress & furs for the first time on Christmas eve [1909,] went to Confession to St. Bernard's Church & went to Mass 7:30 & 8 o'clock on Xmas day. How depressed and lonely I felt, but still I kept up on the following Sunday morning. 26th Dec. Mike & I went to 10:30 Mass to Cathedral, heard a fine sermon preached by Bishop Ireland....

Went to do housework to Mrs. Partridge Sunday 23rd Jan. 1910 felt most unhappy all along but always shaded the clouds. On Monday 31st Feb. [1910] I got sick & felt very poorly all week. Thursday I had to go to bed, I was all a rash of measels. Partridge's house up side down, everybody sick. Was taken in the ambulance to the City Hospital by Dr. Walker on Saturday 5 March 1910. How I felt when I discovered the soiled linen, was there only 4 days when I got an earache, had an ice bag on which was a little relief. About the 9th day I got dyptheria, & never was aware of it until it was all over. Transfered to private room with Lizzie, & our horrible nurse Mrs. Laylor. Oh did I feel. But I had God's assistance all along....

June 1st [1910] came out to the farm with Julies *[Julius Suckow, Louis Hill's "houseman"]* to work for Mrs. Hill, felt very confused for the first week but soon began to like it. Got acquainted with the 1st Japanese boys I ever seen Henry Yosheda & Charley Yomada *[Hill's gardeners, probably brought from his home in Pebble Beach, Calif.]*. How I liked the beautiful boat rides. About 20th June Mrs. took all to town but Charlotte & I, & how glad & happy we were. On Sunday 27th I went to Church to Little Canada in a rig with Mr. Roe & the french sermon I enjoyed. Ida & Charlotte surprised me with all the dainties for dinner & the lovely salad dressing. On Monday 28 I went to town on train & got Mae Wallace her wedding present. Came up to Aunt Mary's & we went down town. Met Annie at Union depot & came on train to Farm, had a dandy time all evening. John Olsen took us boat riding & afterwards played on piano (12 oclock). On Tuesday morning Ida & Charlotte went to town & we had some snap shots taken at front door.

On Saturday 20th July Charlotte & I went on lake all alone. I rowed first time with 2 oars, got along fine, came back about 9 oclock, had some cherries & candy, & Harry & we girls went for a walk up towards the office, smelt something so bad, went along till we met Mr. Webb *[James J. Hill's clerk for North Oaks]*, who advised us to turn back, as there was a skunk around. Gee how it smelt....

On 17th March [1911], Kate & I went down town in the afternoon decorated with the dear old Irish Shamrock, stepped into C. o. C. *[Chamber of Commerce?]* & afterwards went in to see the girls at the Ryan [Hotel]. Mary O'Dowd was out, but Winnie was home, arranged to go to Hastings that night. After supper Kate & I got ready & went down to 7 & Wabasha but no Winnie. Met the crowd at Robert St. walked again up to Wabasha but couldn't see Winnie. Met Mr. Gordley, who was on for the Armory. We all took the Hamline car at Ninth & Wabasha had a fine time all the way out.... Came home at 5:30 and we all had a good time. Annie O'Keefe slipped on car all bleeding. I went to bed for an hour, felt very tired all day Saturday....

On Saturday 8th April Catherine Hendry & Fraulein *[fellow domes-tics; the latter often accompanied Mrs. Hill and the children on trips]* sug-gested I should do the laundry for Mrs. Hill. So brave & gay, I started Monday 10th April. Didn't like it very well to begin with, as I had a bad cold & a sore throat. Continued on the following week & Mrs. wasn't get-ting anybody & I was discouraged, as I didn't have my mind on my work. So on Tuesday April 25th Mrs. came down & asked Kate to stay in the town house & sent for me to do the laundry work. We both have ar-ranged to stay in town for the summer. I wonder how I'll like it but my later pages will tell. On Thursday April 27th Elizabeth took me to Min-neapolis first time, we rode on Selby line, & around by Henipin, we visited all the large stores, I wrote some postals, while Elizabeth wrote a letter, we had supper, & started home at 6:15 P.M. got home at 7:30 & Fraulein had the children in bed. . . .

Mary O'Dowd came 23rd May & stayed till 1st Oct. 1912. The people [Hill family] stayed away till 20th Septr. & we had a big summer. Break-fast at 9 o'clock, sat at table till phone would ring & sometimes talked so much about old country, that we both cried hard. Oh Gee but it was a great summer alright. . . .

Xmas eve [1912] John & I spent in kitchen I felt for the first time since in America very homesick. Xmas day I spent up to Aunt Mary's. Had a pleasant time. John & I went to the show in the evening. New Year's in Auntie Katie's. Mike & I Had a big time, danced & cut up.

Sources for personal account: For background on Irish women immigrants, see Janet A. Nolan, *Ourselves Alone: Women's Emigration from Ireland, 1885-1920*, 2, 32–51 (Lexing-ton, Ky., 1989); Hasia R. Diner, *Erin's Daughters in America: Irish Immigrant Women in the Nineteenth Century* (Baltimore, 1984). On Winnifred Lydon and the Hill family, see Diary of Winnifred Lydon, MHS; Ann Gigrich to Regan, Sept. 5, 2001, notes from inter-view with Ann Gigrich (Lydon's granddaughter), Sept. 18, 2001, and research notes by Shana Redmond, all in People of Minnesota Papers, MHS.

For Further Reading

Hildebrand, John. *Mapping the Farm: The Chronicle of a Family.* New York: Knopf, 1995; St. Paul: Minnesota Historical Society Press, 2001.

Holmquist, June D., ed., *They Chose Minnesota: A Survey of the State's Ethnic Groups* (St. Paul: Minnesota Historical Society Press, 1981).

Johnston, Patricia C. *The Irish in Minnesota.* Afton, Minn.: Johnston Publishing, 1984.

Kenny, Kevin. *The American Irish: A History.* Harlow, England: Longman, 2000.

Miller, Kerby A. *Emigrants and Exiles: Ireland and the Irish Exodus to North America.* New York: Oxford University Press, 1985.

Nolan, Janet. *Ourselves Alone: Women's Emigration from Ireland, 1885–1920.* Lexington: University Press of Kentucky, 1989.

O'Connell, Marvin R. *John Ireland and the American Catholic Church.* St. Paul: Minnesota Historical Society Press, 1988.

Shannon, James P. *Catholic Colonization on the Western Frontier.* New Haven, Conn.: Yale University Press, 1957.

Wingerd, Mary Lethert. *Claiming the City: Politics, Faith, and the Power of Place in St. Paul.* Ithaca, N.Y.: Cornell University Press, 2001.

Notes

1. *St. Paul Pioneer Press*, Feb. 24, 25, 26, 1999, all p. 1.

2. U.S., *Census*, 1860, *Population*, 621; 1870, p. 340; 1880, p. 494; 1890, p. 607.

3. U.S., *Census*, 1940, *Population*, vol. 2, part 1, p. 43, part 4, p. 31; Ann Regan, "The Irish," in June D. Holmquist, ed., *They Chose Minnesota: A Survey of the State's Ethnic Groups*, table 7.1, 131 (St. Paul, 1981).

4. Kerby A. Miller, *Emigrants and Exiles: Ireland and the Irish Exodus to North America*, 21–54 (New York, 1985). Kevin Kenny, *The American Irish: A History* (Harlow, England, 2000), provides a concise overview of Irish immigration that places the periods of Irish immigration in context.

5. Miller, *Emigrants and Exiles*, 50, 291, 346; James S. Donnelly, Jr., *The Great Irish Potato Famine*, 1–11, 171, 278 (Gloucestershire, England, 2001).

6. Here and below, see Miller, *Emigrants and Exiles*, 315, 326–28; Carl Wittke, *The Irish in America*, 62, 114–24 (Baton Rouge, La., 1956); Lawrence J. McCaffrey, *The Irish Catholic Diaspora in America*, 1, 68–71, 93–99 (Washington, D.C., 1997).

7. On Irish migration through, and occupations in, the Midwest, see Sister Mary Gilbert Kelly, *Catholic Immigrant Colonization Projects in the United States, 1815–1860*, 26, 31, 106, 147–50, 179, 204–6 (United States Catholic Historical Society, Monograph Series XVII—New York, 1939); Sister Mary Evangela Henthorne, *The Irish Catholic Colonization Association of the United States*, 31 (Champaign,

Ill., 1932); David E. Schob, *Hired Hands and Plowboys: Farm Labor in the Midwest, 1815–60*, 117 (Urbana, Ill., 1975); Sister M. Justine McDonald, *History of the Irish in Wisconsin in the Nineteenth Century*, 47 (Washington, D.C., 1954); Jim Rees, *A Farewell to Famine* (Arklow, Ireland, 1994).

8. In 1870 about half of the Irish families in Eagan and Burnsville Townships, Dakota County, and Credit River and Cedar Lake Townships, Scott County, had children who were born in Canada or states other than Minnesota. For other examples of staged migration, see biographies published in Mary L. Hagerty, *Meet Shieldsville: The Story of St. Patrick's Parish Shieldsville, Minnesota*, 77–167 ([Shieldsville, 1940]); James E. Child, *Child's History of Waseca County, Minnesota*, 669–808 (Owatonna, 1905). On migration through Canada, see Brian Clarke, "Canadian Irish/ American Irish," in Michael Glazier, ed., *The Encyclopedia of the Irish in America*, 109 (Notre Dame, Ind., 1999); Cecil Woodham-Smith, *The Great Hunger*, 211–217 (London, 1962). Malcolm Campbell found a similar pattern of staged migration and successful adaptation in his study comparing Minnesota's rural Irish to Irish settlers in New South Wales, Australia, "Immigrants on the Land: Irish Rural Settlement in Minnesota and New South Wales, 1830–1890," *New Hibernia Review*, 2: 43–61 (Spring 1998).

9. Bruce M. White and Helen M. White, "Fort Snelling 1838: An Ethnographic and Historical Study," a report

prepared for the Historic Sites Department, Minnesota Historical Society (hereafter MHS), 1998; J. Fletcher Williams, *A History of the City of St. Paul to 1875*, 70–73, 90–93 (St. Paul, 1876, 1983); Gustavus Otto to his wife, April 7, 1849, as quoted in Francis P. Prucha, "An Army Private at Old Fort Snelling in 1849," in *Minnesota History*, 36:17 (March 1958). Hays was later murdered, probably by Phelan, who was not convicted. Phelan took a claim in what is now St. Paul's East Side, where a popular city park is named for him, although it is spelled differently.

10. Hand count of Minnesota manuscript census schedules, 1850, in Minnesota Ethnic History Project (hereafter MEHP) Papers, MHS; Kelly, *Catholic Immigrant Colonization Projects*, 35; Agnes M. Larson, *Lumbering in the Last of the White Pine States*, 76 (Minneapolis, 1949).

11. Here and in the next paragraph, see Joseph A. King, *The Irish Lumberman Farmer: Fitzgeralds, Harrigans and Others*, 112, 114–16, 120, 137–42, 230–32 (Lafayette, Calif., 1982); *Stillwater Lumberman*, Apr. 23, 1875 (quotation); Catholic Archdiocese of St. Paul and Minneapolis, Parish Questionnaires, Stillwater (St. Michael) and Mora (St. Mary), 1948, originals in the Catholic Historical Society, St. Paul Seminary, microfilm in MHS, hereafter cited as Parish Questionnaires; Patricia C. Harpole and Mary D. Nagle, *Minnesota Territorial Census, 1850* (St. Paul, 1972). For examples of Irish farmers from New Brunswick in Washington County, see Augustus B. Easton, *History of the St. Croix Valley*, 1: 294, 373, 414, 436, 480 (Chicago, 1909).

12. Kelly, *Catholic Colonization*, 154–55, 164; Thomas E. Auge, "The Dream of Bishop Loras: A Catholic Iowa," in *Palimpsest*, 61: 170–79 (1980); Margaret E. Hutcheson, *125th Anniversary: St. Columbkill Catholic Church*, 4 ([Belle Creek, 1985?]). In the 1850s the *Boston Pilot*, a widely circulated Catholic paper, printed many stories about Irish settlers in Minnesota, Wisconsin, and Iowa. A list of the articles is enclosed in A. F. Mace to Most Rev. John Ireland, Mar. 5, 1897, MHS.

13. Rhoda R. Gilman, "How Minnesota Became the 32nd State," in *Minnesota History*, 56: 158, 160–62, 164 (Winter 1998–99).

14. From 1860 U.S. manuscript census schedules, tabulations in MEHP Papers. For more on these communities, see *Irish Gazette*, Feb. 1993, p. 3 (Jessenland); John G. Berger, *A History of St. Brendan's Parish, the Village of Green Isle, and Minnesota's First Irish Settlement* (n.p., 1968).

15. On communities, see 1860 U.S. manuscript census schedules, tabulations in MEHP Papers; William J. Casey, *A History of Cedar Lake Township Scott County Minnesota* ([Jordan], 1939); Harold Albrecht, *This Is Our Town*, 573–83 ([Belle Plaine, 1977]); Gerald Mattson, *Church on the Seven Mile Prairie: An Early History of St. Joseph's Parish and the Times and Lives of Its First Parishioners*, 15–16 ([Rosemount], 1982); John D. O'Connell, *The Log Church in Derrynane* ([Shakopee, 1946]); Berger, *History of St. Brendan's Parish*; Sister Mary Zaccheus Ryan, *Irish Roots*, 9 (Faribault, 1980). On the Dodd Road, most of which survives as county roads, see Grover Singley, *Tracing Minnesota's Old Government Roads*, 39, 41–45 (St. Paul, 1974); Ralph H. Bowen, ed., *A Frontier Family in Minnesota: Letters of Theodore and Sophie Bost, 1851–1920*, 34, 44, 47 (Minneapolis, 1981). Bost, a Swiss immigrant, described the difficulty of su-

pervising the Irish laborers whom Dodd had hired: "They hate all overseers, and the latter have to be continually on their guard; sometimes they [the Irish] take it into their heads to beat up a supervisor" (p. 34).

16. Parish Questionnaires; 1860 U.S. manuscript census schedules, tabulations in MEHP Papers; Carol Walhovd and Fern Heller, *The Brownsville Story,* 58 (Winona, 1976); Joel Sobel, "The Urban Frontier Labor Force: Structure and Persistence in Three Nineteenth Century Minnesota Towns," 19, 136, 171, Ph.D. thesis, University of Minnesota, 1978. The Irish population of Hastings was, for its size, overrepresented in the unskilled labor force.

17. "Southeastern Minnesota" here consists of Blue Earth, Carver, Dakota, Dodge, Faribault, Fillmore, Freeborn, Goodhue, Houston, Le Sueur, Mower, Nicollet, Olmsted, Rice, Scott, Sibley, Steele, Wabasha, Waseca, and Winona Counties. U.S., *Census,* 1870, *Population,* 719–65; 1880, p. 808–54; 1890, vol. 2, p. 530–627; 1900, *Special Reports: Occupations,* 220–422. By 1890 the Irish populations of Minnesota, Wisconsin, Iowa, Kansas, Nebraska, North Dakota, South Dakota, and Oklahoma were nearly or more than 50% agricultural. In absolute terms, however, the numbers were small: Irish agricultural workers in those states totaled 35,701, only 2% of the nation's Irish population.

18. Henry A. Castle, "General James Shields," in *Minnesota Historical Collections,* 15: 719 (St. Paul, 1915); Hagerty, *Meet Shieldsville,* 9, 10, 18; Kelly, *Catholic Immigrant Colonization Projects,* 199, 201; Johanna M. O'Leary, *Historical Sketch of the Parish of the Immaculate Conception,*

Faribault, Minnesota, 11 (Faribault, 1938); L. E. Swanberg, *Then and Now: A History of Rice County, Faribault and Communities,* 248, 261–68, 285 ([Faribault, 1976]); *Northfield News,* May 19, 1933, p. 3 (quotation). On Kilkenny and Montgomery Townships, see Mae Z. Mach, *Remember When: A History of Kilkenny, Minnesota* ([Kilkenny, 1979]); Montgomery Bicentennial Committee, *Montgomery: From the "Big Woods" to the Kolacky Capital, 1856–1976* (Montgomery, 1976). In *Hibernia America: The Irish and Regional Cultures,* 120 (Westport, Conn., 1986), Dennis Clark erroneously asserts that the colony was unsuccessful and the townships were "little more than ghost towns," further promulgating the image of the Irish as unsuccessful farmers.

19. Frank B. Lamson, comp., *Condensed History of Meeker County, 1855–1939,* 90 ([Litchfield, 1939]); Parish Questionnaires, Maple Lake, Birch Cooley, Bird Island, Fairfax, Franklin; Franklyn Curtiss-Wedge, *The History of Renville County, Minnesota,* 2: 1292 (Chicago, 1916); *Irish Gazette,* Mar. 1990, p. 7 (Birch Cooley); Edna M. Busch, *History of Stevens Co.,* 5 (n.p., 1976); Alexius Hoffman, "Natural History of Stearns County," 115, typed manuscript, 1934, in St. John's Abbey Archives, Collegeville; "Past to Present: A History of the Church of St. Donatus, Brooten, Minnesota," undated photocopy in Stearns County Historical Society, St. Cloud; Daisy E. Hughes, *Builders of Pope County,* 26 ([Glenwood], 1930); 1870 and 1880 U.S. manuscript census schedules, Westline Township, Redwood County, and Birch Cooley Township, Renville County.

20. *St. Paul Daily Press,* Sept. 28, 1862; *Duluth Minnesotian,* May 8, 1869; Irving

Caswell, "Pioneer Days at Coon Creek," in *Anoka County Union*, Jan. 1, 1941, p. 7; Vincent A. Yzermans, *The Mel and the Rose*, 299 (Melrose, 1972); U.S., *Census*, 1880, *Population*, 715.

21. Le Sueur Bicentennial Book Committee, *Le Sueur: Town on the River*, 179 ([Le Sueur], 1977); Parish Questionnaires; Charles Zopf, "The History of the Church of St. Louis, Paynesville, Minnesota," [1], (1964), copy in Central Minnesota Historical Center, St. Cloud State University; Yzermans, *The Mel and the Rose*, 302. On divisions, see, for example, Melrose (St. Boniface), Glencoe (St. George and Sts. Peter and Paul), Mankato (St. John the Baptist), and Hastings (Guardian Angel). On much later difficulties in reuniting a split congregation in Caledonia, see *Minneapolis Tribune*, June 11, 1979, p. 2B.

22. Marvin R. O'Connell, *John Ireland and the American Catholic Church*, 9, 35, 68, 134, 218, 255 (St. Paul, 1988).

23. Thomas D. O'Brien, "Dillon O'Brien," in *Acta et Dicta*, 6: 38, 41 (Oct. 1941); James P. Shannon, *Catholic Colonization on the Western Frontier*, 24, 44, 54 (New Haven, Conn., 1957), compares the Minnesota colonies to other western colonization projects. The only surviving copy of the Minnesota Irish Immigration Society's founding circular is enclosed in A. D. McSweeney to Ignatius Donnelly, Oct. 11, 1864, in Ignatius Donnelly Papers, MHS.

24. Shannon, *Catholic Colonization*, 47, 54, 59.

25. Shannon, *Catholic Colonization*, 264.

26. Shannon, *Catholic Colonization*, 52, 135, 151. For example, St. Mary's Church in Lake City was greatly depleted in 1878 when many parishioners left for lands in western Minnesota; Parish Questionnaires.

27. Shannon, *Catholic Colonization*, 88–91, 264; O'Connell, *John Ireland*, 138; Jon Gjerde, *The Minds of the West: Ethnocultural Evolution in the Rural Middle West, 1830–1917*, 12–13, 285 (Chapel Hill, N.C., 1997).

28. Shannon, *Catholic Colonization*, 81, 108–14, 182; John Sweetman, "The Sweetman Catholic Colony of Currie, Minnesota: A Memoir," in *Acta et Dicta*, 3: 61–65 (July 1911); Alice E. Smith, "The Sweetman Irish Colony," in *Minnesota History*, 9: 331–46 (Dec. 1929). The Adrian Colony Papers are in the St. Paul Seminary Archives; Sweetman's Irish-Catholic Colonization Company, Ltd., Papers are in MHS.

29. Shannon, *Catholic Colonization*, 155–65; *St. Paul Globe*, Apr. 4, 1881, Mar. 16, 1902, p. 7; Richard Berg, *The History of St. Michael's Parish*, 15 ([St. Paul, 1966]); Nels M. Hokanson, "I Remember St. Paul's Swede Hollow," in *Minnesota History*, 41: 365, 369 (Winter 1969); Works Projects Administration, Writers' Program, *The Bohemian Flats*, 13 (Minneapolis, [1941]). Connemara Patch is depicted in Sanborn Map and Publishing Co., *St. Paul 1885*, map 7 (New York, 1885). This account is informed by Bridget Connelly, *Forgetting Ireland*, forthcoming from MHS Press.

30. *St. Paul Pioneer Press*, Dec. 22, 1880; Shannon, *Catholic Colonization*, 165; O'Brien, "Dillon O'Brien," and Humphrey Moynihan, "Archbishop Ireland's Colonies," in *Acta et Dicta*, 6: 51, 222 (Oct. 1933, Oct. 1934).

31. Kittson County Historical Society, *Our Northwest Corner: History of Kittson County, Minnesota*, 4, 495, 588 (Dallas,

1976); *Our Northland Diocese* (Crookston), Golden Jubilee edition, Sept. 1960, p. 13; Hiram M. Drache, *The Day of the Bonanza: A History of Bonanza Farming in the Red River Valley of the North*, 113 (Fargo, N.Dak., 1964); Knut Hamsun, "On the Prairie: A Sketch of the Red River Valley," in *Minnesota History*, 37: 266 (Sept. 1961). About half of the 20 men in the bonanza farm crew Hamsun described were Irish.

32. On Irish born, see Joseph Stipanovich, "The Report of the Iron Range Historical-Cultural Survey," 168, 173, 205 (Sept. 1979), copy in MHS; John Sirjamaki, "The People of the Mesabi Range," in *Minnesota History*, 27: 205, 208, 210 (Sept. 1946); George O. Virtue, *The Minnesota Iron Ranges*, 345, 353 (United States Bureau of Labor, Bulletin no. 84— Washington, D.C., 1909). On American born, see Minnesota, *Census, 1905*, 197, 199; *Eveleth News-Clarion*, July 31, 1947, sec. 1, p. 8; Clarke A. Chambers, "Social Welfare Policies and Programs on the Minnesota Iron Range, 1880–1930," 18–22, typed paper, 1963, copy in MHS.

33. Minnesota, *Census, 1895*, 192; author's analysis of Sacred Heart Cathedral and St. Clement's parishes, from *Catholic Directory of Duluth and Almanac for 1892*, 1–58, 73–84 (Duluth, 1892), in MEHP Papers; *Duluth Daily News*, Mar. 18, 1892; *Duluth Herald*, June 7, 1965, p. 9. No occupations were given for 107 males and 24 single females; only 186 married females were listed. Irish surnames were identified with the help of Edward MacLysaght, *A Guide to Irish Surnames* (Baltimore, 1964). A separate tabulation for 358 parishioners with Scottish and English names, some of whom were undoubtedly Irish, revealed a lower proportion of un-skilled laborers (23.6%) and correspondingly higher proportions of white-collar workers (24.3%) among males and a higher proportion (32.1%) of office workers among females.

34. U.S., *Census, 1910, Population*, 1: 841; 1920, vol. 2, p. 959, 961.

35. U.S., *Census, 1890, Population*, 1: 607, 671. In 1890 St. Paul's German-born population was more than twice that of the Irish born.

36. Lucile M. Kane and Alan Ominsky, *Twin Cities: A Pictorial History of St. Paul and Minneapolis*, 6–7 (St. Paul, 1983). The discussion of St. Paul's Irish identity, below, relies heavily on the insightful work of Mary Lethert Wingerd, *Claiming the City: Politics, Faith, and the Power of Place in St. Paul* (Ithaca, N.Y., 2001).

37. James K. Benson, "New England of the West: The Emergence of American Mind in Early St. Paul, Minnesota, 1849–1850," 60, master's thesis, University of Minnesota, 1970; Daniel J. Fisher to B. J. McQuaid, [1852], in *Acta et Dicta*, 1: 45 (July 1907).

38. *Daily Minnesotian*, June 5, 1857; *Minnesota Republican* (St. Anthony), Mar. 19, 1858. For other notes of irregularity at the polls, see *Daily Minnesotian*, May 7, 1857, *Minnesota Weekly Times*, May 6, 1857.

39. *Minnesota Democrat* (St. Paul), Mar. 21, 1855; *St. Paul City Directory*, 1856–57, p. 22, 23; Benson, "New England of the West," 77; *St. Paul Pioneer Press*, July 17, 1856.

40. Cretin to Bishop Mathias Loras, Mar. 10, 1853, quoted in M. M. Hoffman, *The Church Founders of the Northwest*, 333 (Milwaukee, 1937); Parish Questionnaires.

41. Calvin Schmid, *Social Saga of Two Cities: An Ecological and Statistical Study*,

chart 88 (Minneapolis, 1937); Minnesota Emergency Relief Administration, *Foreign Born Population Studies: St. Paul, Minnesota,* [29] (St. Paul, 1934); Minnesota, *Census, 1895,* 187, *1905,* 171. The second and third generations, many of whom may have moved to the cities from farming areas, disappear in these statistics. It is thus impossible to measure the size of the group that was identified by surname as Irish in later years.

42. Kathleen O'Brien, "Irish in Minneapolis," [12–16], typed paper, 1973, copy in MEHP Papers; Herman E. Olson, *The Minneapolis Property and Housing Survey,* p. 1 of sections on Wards 1–13 (Minneapolis, 1934); Parish Questionnaires.

43. U.S., *Census,* 1880, *Population,* 887; O'Brien, "Irish in Minneapolis," [26, 68]. O'Brien's figures are based on a random sample of households with Irish-born members. The 1880 census, which counted only Irish born, gave 31% of that population as laborers. For other figures on Minneapolis Irish occupations, see U.S., *Census,* 1890, *Population,* part 2, p. 694; 1900, *Special Reports: Occupations,* 614–17. Those for 1880 and 1890 included only first generation; for 1900 total foreign stock was given, listing each sex separately. Some Minneapolis Swedes resented Irish domination of public jobs. See *Svenska Amerikanska Posten* (Minneapolis), Feb. 7, May 9, Dec. 26, 1893.

44. Here and below, see U.S., *Census,* 1880, *Population,* 901; 1890, part 2, p. 726; 1900, *Special Reports: Occupations,* 710–15; Wingerd, *Claiming the City,* 45. The Butlers were the general contractors for Minnesota's state capitol, built in 1905, and the Shielys were subcontractors. See Neil B. Thompson, *Minnesota's State Capitol: The Art and Politics of a Public Building,*

31, 39 (St. Paul, 1974). On the Butler family, which became deeply involved in contracting and iron mining and also produced several lawyers and a U.S. Supreme Court justice, see *Northwest Life,* Jan. 29, 1946, p. 18–20; on other Irish contractors, see Joseph L. Shiely, "Giants with the Earth," 1, 10, 14, 19, typed manuscript, 1958, in MHS. For more on the occupations of Irish women in America, see Janet Nolan, *Ourselves Alone: Women's Emigration from Ireland, 1885–1920* (Lexington, Ky., 1989).

45. [Alix J. Muller and Frank J. Meade], *History of the Police and Fire Departments of the Twin Cities,* St. Paul, 46, 58 (Minneapolis and St. Paul, [1899]); Kieran D. Flanagan, "Immigration, Assimilation, and Occupational Patterns of the St. Paul Irish," 246, 250, master's thesis, University of Minnesota, 1969. In Minneapolis early proportions of Irish policemen were lower, but by 1900, 25% of the city's protective service workers were Irish; U.S., *Census,* 1900, *Special Reports: Occupations,* 614.

46. Minneapolis mayor A. C. Rand defended a similar system in his city in 1881, noting that two-thirds of the fines levied upon Minneapolis' disorderly houses went to support Bethany Home, a private charity. [Muller and Meade], *History of the Police and Fire Departments,* St. Paul, 62, Minneapolis, 47; *Souvenir Book of the Saint Paul Police Department,* [25] (St. Paul, 1904). On Christopher O'Brien, see Thomas D. O'Brien, *There Were Four of Us or, Was It Five,* 19 (St. Paul, 1936); *St. Paul Daily News,* Jan. 10, 1933, p. 2.

47. Wittke, *Irish in America,* 233; William V. Shannon, *The American Irish,* 11 (New York, 1963); U.S., *Census,* 1880, *Population,* 901, and *Special Reports: Occupa-*

tions, 710–15. On the O'Brien family, see O'Brien, *There Were Four of Us.*

48. Wingerd, *Claiming the City*, 29–38. On Minneapolis and labor, see William Millikan, *A Union against Unions: The Minneapolis Citizens Alliance and Its Fight against Organized Labor, 1903–1947* (St. Paul, 2000).

49. Horace S. Merrill, "Ignatius Donnelly, James J. Hill, and Cleveland Administration Patronage," in *Mississippi Valley Historical Review*, 39: 508, 515 (Dec. 1952); *St. Paul Pioneer Press*, May 2, 1894; Horace S. Merrill, *Bourbon Democracy of the Middle West*, 2 (Baton Rouge, La., 1953). On Murray, see Warren Upham and Rose B. Dunlap, eds., *Minnesota Biographies, 1655–1912*, 535 (St. Paul, 1912), and Thomas M. Newson, *Pen Pictures of St. Paul*, 149 (St. Paul, 1886); on Kelly, see *St. Paul Pioneer Press*, Oct. 24, 1900, p. 1; on Doran, see *Belle Plaine Herald*, Feb. 25, 1915, p. 1.

50. Wingerd, *Claiming the City*, 41–46, 53, 56–57, 106–7.

51. O'Connell, *John Ireland*, 378, 382; Wingerd, *Claiming the City*, 45, 87, 99.

52. *St. Paul Pioneer Press*, Aug. 11, 1930, p. 1, Oct. 18, 1953 (on aperture card 10734, reference room, St. Paul Public Library); *St. Paul Daily News*, Jan. 9, p. 1; 10, p. 1; 11, p. 7; 12, p. 5; 13, p. 2; 22, sec. 1, p. 5—all 1933; *St. Paul Dispatch*, July 4, 1924, p. 1; W. B. Hennessy, *Past and Present of St. Paul, Minnesota*, 579, 753 (Chicago, 1909). The *Daily News* articles were part of "The Life of Dick O'Connor," by George C. Rogers, printed serially from Jan. 9 to Feb. 2, 1933.

53. Paul Maccabee, *John Dillinger Slept Here: A Crooks' Tour of Crime and Corruption in St. Paul, 1920–1936*, 2–12, 78, 148, 192, 250–59 (St. Paul, 1995). An exposé of the collapsing system was printed in the *St. Paul Daily News*, June 24 to July 20, 1935.

54. Wingerd, *Claiming the City*, 111 ("labels"), 112 ("defining feature"), 113.

55. On Donnelly, see Martin Ridge, *Ignatius Donnelly: The Portrait of a Politician* (Chicago, 1962; St. Paul, 1991). For an example of Irish orations, see *The Irish-American Banquet to the Earl of Aberdeen*, 21–31 ([St. Paul], 1887), copy in MHS.

56. James Manahan, *Trials of a Lawyer* ([St. Paul, 1933]); Carl H. Chrislock, *The Progressive Era in Minnesota, 1899–1918*, 19, 51, 149 (St. Paul, 1971). Manahan's papers, containing personal, professional, and political correspondence, are in MHS. Many letters demonstrate the interconnections among St. Paul's Irish politicians.

57. Eugene P. Wiliging and Herta Hatzfeld, *Catholic Serials of the Nineteenth Century in the United States: A Descriptive Bibliography and Union List*, 24, 41–43 (2nd series, part 1—Washington, D.C., 1959). Other Irish Catholic papers printed in Minnesota were the *Irish Times* (St. Paul, 1872–?), *Western Times* (St. Paul, 1872–74), *Celtic World* (Minneapolis, 1881–82), and *National Hibernian* (St. Paul, 1892–95). MHS has some issues of all but the last of these.

58. *St. Paul Pioneer*, Mar. 20, 1866.

59. William D'Arcy, *The Fenian Movement in the United States: 1858–1886*, 15 (Washington, D.C., 1947); Joseph K. Howard, *Strange Empire: A Narrative of the Northwest*, 217–21 (1952; Reprint ed., St. Paul, 1994); *St. Paul Press*, June 7, 1866; Phillip E. Myers, "The Fenians in Iowa," in *Palimpsest*, 62: 56, 57 (1981); John P. Pritchett, "The Origin of the So-Called Fenian Raid on Manitoba in 1871," in *Canadian Historical Review*, 10: 32–42 (Mar. 1929); *St. Paul Pioneer*, Oct. 12, Nov. 16, 20 (United

Irishmen), 1871; *St. Paul Globe,* Nov. 18, 1871, Dec. 7, 1902, p. 24. For newspaper reaction to the rumors, see *Minneapolis Tribune,* May 19, 1870; *St. Paul Dispatch,* May 28, 1870; *St. Cloud Journal,* June 16, 1870. On Nov. 8, 1864, the *St. Paul Pioneer* reprinted a speech delivered to "the Fenian Sisterhood of St. Paul." No other evidence of this group has been located.

60. *St. Paul Pioneer Press,* Aug. 3, 1877.

61. *St. Paul Globe,* Feb. 27, 1880; *Northwestern Chronicle,* Feb. 21, 28, 1880. Bishop Grace decreed that the collections from the services of Feb. 29, 1880, were to be sent for Irish relief. A benefit in Stillwater on Mar. 13 brought pledges of $800; Minneapolis Irish canceled their St. Patrick's Day parade "on account of the distress across the water." See *St. Paul Dispatch,* Feb. 27, 1880; *St. Paul Globe,* Mar. 13, 1880; *Minneapolis Tribune,* Mar. 6, 1880. Records of pledges from Irish communities in southern Minnesota are printed in *Northwestern Chronicle,* Feb. 28, 1880. See also William G. Van Horn and the Irish National Land League to S. Freidlander, July 9, 1880, MHS, signed by Parnell and six other Land League officials.

62. *Northwestern Chronicle,* Nov. 22, 1883; *St. Paul Daily Pioneer,* Jan. 11, 1874; *Stillwater Gazette,* Jan. 20, 1875; *St. Paul Globe,* Mar. 3, 1878, June 1, 1880.

63. Hibernians of Minnesota, *From Ireland to Minnesota,* 20–22, 66–70, 73–76 (St. Paul, 1996) (hereafter Hibernians, *From Ireland*); interview of Leah Curtin by author, Jan. 24, 1980, notes in MEHP Papers; *St. Paul Pioneer Press,* July 26, 1996, p. 2D.

64. James M. Reardon, "The Catholic Total Abstinence Movement in Minnesota," in *Acta et Dicta,* 2: 46, 48 (July 1909); *Minneapolis Tribune,* Sept. 26, 1918, p. 8;

Charles J. Carmody, "Rechabites in Purple: A History of the Catholic Temperance Movement in the Northwest," 60, master's thesis, St. Paul Seminary, 1953.

65. Reardon, in *Acta et Dicta,* 2: 55, 85; Carmody, "Rechabites in Purple," 171; *St. Paul Pioneer Press,* Aug. 2, 1882. Ireland lectured on temperance across the United States, earning for himself the title "Father Mathew of the Northwest." For examples of his temperance rhetoric, see *St. Paul Pioneer,* Apr. 23, 1869, Aug. 3, 1882; "Intemperance and Law," in John Ireland, *The Church and Modern Society,* 1: 259–308 (St. Paul, 1904).

66. Carmody, "Rechabites in Purple," 99, 134, 144, 162; Reardon, in *Acta et Dicta,* 2: 58, 71, 83, 85, 91.

67. O'Connell, *John Ireland,* 106–14; Wingerd, *Claiming the City,* 99–100; Sister Joan Bland, *Hibernian Crusade: The Story of the Catholic Total Abstinence Union of America,* 8 (Washington, D.C., 1951); Carmody, "Rechabites in Purple," 120, 157, 174; *Minneapolis Tribune,* Sept. 26, 1918, p. 7; "The Catholic Church and the Saloon," in Ireland, *Church and Modern Society,* 1: 309–25.

68. *St. Paul Pioneer Press,* Aug. 4, 1882. For other evaluations, see Reardon, in *Acta et Dicta,* 2: 85, 92; Carmody, "Rechabites in Purple," 155; William W. Folwell, *A History of Minnesota,* 2: 98 (Reprint ed., St. Paul, 1961); *St. Paul Daily Press,* May 2, 1873. All are laudatory.

69. O'Connell, *John Ireland,* 217–19; Colman J. Barry, *The Catholic Church and German Americans,* 118 (Milwaukee, 1953); Daniel P. O'Neill, "St. Paul Priests, 1851–1930: Recruitment, Formation, and Mobility," 138, Ph.D. thesis, University of Minnesota, 1979.

70. *Minnesota Democrat,* Mar. 22, 1854.

For the first notice of a St. Patrick's Day celebration in St. Paul, see *St. Paul Pioneer,* Mar. 20, 1851.

71. See, for example, *Northwestern Chronicle,* Mar. 21, 1868, Mar. 20, 1869; *St. Paul Daily Press,* Mar. 19, 1861; *St. Paul Globe,* Mar. 18, 1880. On Ireland's speeches, see Charles J. O'Fahey, "John Ireland's Rhetorical Vision of the Irish in America," 44–47, master's thesis, University of Minnesota, 1973, and "Reflections on the St. Patrick's Day Orations of John Ireland," in *Ethnicity,* 2: 249–54 (1975).

72. *Northwestern Chronicle,* Mar. 13, 1869; *St. Paul Daily Globe,* Mar. 17, 1880.

73. *St. Paul Pioneer and Democrat,* Mar. 20, 1860; on St. Vincent's, see Wingerd, *Claiming the City,* 108.

74. *Northwestern Chronicle,* Mar. 23, 1867, Mar. 13, 1875; *Irish Standard,* Mar. 23, 1901, p. 1; *Winona Independent,* Mar. 17, 1909, p. 4.

75. *Irish Standard,* Mar. 21, 1903, p. 5; *St. Paul City Directory,* 1920, 661, 1923, 597; *St. Paul Dispatch,* Aug. 30, 1922, p. 1. Irish groups mentioned in the *St. Paul Pioneer Press* during these years included the Irish Benevolent Association of St. Paul (Mar. 12, 1910, p. 12), Shamrock Club (Mar. 17, 1911, p. 7), Minneapolis Sinn Fein Club (May 22, 1911, p. 8), Loyal Sons of Erin (Mar. 18, 1932, p. 1), and Friendly Sons of St. Patrick (Sept. 4, 1949, sec. 1, p. 3).

76. *Irish Standard,* Oct. 31, 1914, p. 1, Nov. 6, 1914, p. 6, Apr. 13, 1915, p. 1, Oct. 27, 1917, p. 1, Nov. 10, 1917, p. 1; Wingerd, *Claiming the City,* 133–34; "Three Minutes of Practical Americanism. Pro-German Sinn Fein Propaganda Menaces America" [1917?], flier signed by seven prominent Irish St. Paulites, in Louis W. Hill Papers, James J. Hill Library, St. Paul. The vilification of Germans during the war ended many German cultural activities in St. Paul, further boosting the profile of the Irish; Wingerd, *Claiming the City,* 210–11. For examples of activities, see *St. Paul Pioneer Press,* Mar. 12, 1910, p. 12; May 23, 1911, p. 10; *Minneapolis Journal,* Mar. 3, 1918, p. 10; interview of John Curtin by author, Nov. 1, 1980, notes in MEHP Papers. For an example of a bond in the Irish Republic, see Miscellaneous Printed Materials, William Mahoney Papers, MHS.

77. *St. Paul Pioneer Press,* Mar. 17, 1920, p. 6; "Mayors of St. Paul," reference aid, MHS.

78. Millard L. Gieske, *Minnesota Farmer-Laborism: The Third Party Alternative,* 224, 287, 291, 296, 325 (Minneapolis, 1979); John Earl Haynes, *Dubious Alliance: The Making of Minnesota's DFL Party,* 66–68 (Minneapolis, 1984).

79. Hibernians, *From Ireland,* 95; John Curtin interview, Nov. 1, 1980; Alan Altshuler, *A Report on Politics in St. Paul,* part 1, p. 5 (Cambridge, Mass., 1959); *Minneapolis Star Tribune,* Mar. 17, 1986, p. 1A.

80. Andrew Greeley, "Achievements of the Irish in America," Patrick K. Blessing, "Irish in America," and James Silas Rogers, "St. Paul and Minneapolis" and "Minnesota," in Glazier, ed., *Encyclopedia of the Irish in America* 1–4, 466–69, 611–14, 822–24.

81. U.S., *Census,* 1900, *Population,* 2: 521, 1990, Minnesota, *Social and Economic Characteristics,* 11. For examples of suburban encroachment, see sidebar on Cahill, p. 55; interview of Enous Gallagher by Ann Regan, Apr. 28, 1980, tape at MHS; *St. Paul Pioneer Press,* Aug. 13, 2001, p. 1. The Agricultural Society's Century Farms Project Application Forms, 1976–1985, are in Minnesota State Archives, MHS. Plat books

checked include Rockford Map Publishers, *Land Atlas and Plat Book Dakota County Minnesota, 1997*, and 1997 directories published by Farm and Home Publishers for Houston, Le Sueur, Rice, Scott, and Sibley Counties. On parades, see *New Ulm Journal*, Mar. 11, 2001; interview with *Belle Plaine Herald*, Mar. 11, 1998, p. 1; *Minneapolis Star and Tribune*, Mar. 17, 1987, p. 1C, Mar. 17, 1999, p. 1B; interview with Dee Wolf, Aug. 21, 2001; *Waseca Journal*, Mar. 17, 1969, p. 1. One Irish family's tenure on a farm near Rochester since 1879 is powerfully depicted in John Hildebrand, *Mapping the Farm: The Chronicle of a Family* (New York, 1995; St. Paul, 2001).

82. Interview of Michael Whalen by author, Nov. 2, 1980, notes in MEHP Papers; interview of Steve O'Neill, Sept. 25, 2001; *Duluth News Tribune*, Mar. 18, 1975, p. 11, Mar. 18, 1978, p. 6A, Mar. 10, 2001, Wave section, p. 10–13. The parade ended after 1996.

83. Kenny, *American Irish*, 230; *St. Paul Pioneer Press*, Mar. 17, 1990, p. 1A, Oct. 22, 1990, p. 1B, Mar. 19, 1994, p. 1D; *Minneapolis Star and Tribune*, Mar. 17, 1989.

84. U.S., *Census*, 1990, Minnesota, *Social and Economic Characteristics*, 81; University of Minnesota Map Library, on-line Atlas of Minnesota, www-map.lib.umn. edu/bessie/irish.

85. For Irish Northern Aid, see Hibernians, *From Ireland*, 93; for Unity Conference, see *Irish Gazette*, Jan.–Feb. 2001, p. 10; Hibernians, *From Ireland*, 93; for United Ireland, see Hibernians, *From Ireland*, 88; *Irish Gazette*, Mar. 1997, p. 5; for Children's Program, see *Irish Gazette*, Dec. 1997, p. 2, Aug. 1999, p. 3, Aug. 2001, p. 18; *Brainerd Dispatch*, July 25, 1998; *Star Tribune*, June 27, 2001, 1B.

86. For AOH, see Hibernians, *From Ireland*, 20–22, 66–70, 73–76; interview with Leah Curtin, Aug. 21, 2001; for Genealogical Society, see http://www.rootsweb. com/~irish; for Gaeltacht Minnesota, see Hibernians, *From Ireland*, 91–92; for Failte Minnesota, see *Irish Gazette*, Mar./Apr. 2001, p. 20, Aug./Sept. 2001, p. 4; interview with Maxine Keoghan, Aug. 20, 2001; for Irish Books and Media, see *Irish Gazette*, Mar./Apr. 1998, p. 8; Hibernians, *From Ireland*, 92; for Irish Gazette, see *Irish Gazette*, Aug./Sept. 2001; for Emerald Society, see Hibernians, *From Ireland*, 90; for Na Fianna, see *Irish Gazette*, Mar. 1990, p. 3, Mar. 1991, p. 13, Mar. 1992, p. 10; Hibernians, *From Ireland*, 93–94.

87. Hibernians, *From Ireland*, 87; *Star Tribune*, Mar. 14, 1996, p. B3; *St. Paul Pioneer Press*, June 29, 1997, p. 5E.

88. For IMDA (originally a chapter of Comhaltus Ceoltoiri Eireann), see Hibernians, *From Ireland*, 88; interview with Virginia McBride, May 28, 2001; for Studios and groups, see "IMDA Irish Community Resource List, 2001"; Marisa Helms, "Central Minnesota's Irish Connection," Aug. 10, 2000, Minnesota Public Radio; *Irish Gazette*, Mar. 1997, p. 7; for Pipe bands, see Hibernians, *From Ireland*, 90–91; Sam Dillon, "Pumping Irish in St. Paul," in *Sweet Potato* (Minneapolis), May 1980, p. 13 for Musicians, see *St. Paul Pioneer Press*, Mar. 16, 2001, p. 2E.

89. Hibernians, *From Ireland*, 84–85; *St. Paul Pioneer Press*, Nov. 13, 1980, Aug. 13, 2001, p. 4B; Curtin interview, Aug. 21, 2001.

90. *Star Tribune*, Mar. 18, 2001, p. 3B; *Irish Gazette*, Mar. 1991, p. 1.

91. Marilyn Halter, a scholar of ethnicity, argues that immigrants abandoned the material culture of the homeland in order to become American, and now their

descendants, lost in a mass commercial culture, buy and consume ethnic goods to proclaim their individuality; see Halter, *Shopping for Identity: The Marketing of Ethnicity*, 7–10, 161 (New York, 2000). I am indebted to James Rogers for this reference and the insight.

Notes to Sidebars

The Protestant Irish, p. 2: These paragraphs first appeared in Sarah P. Rubinstein, "The British," in Holmquist, ed., *They Chose Minnesota*, 118–19. They are based on James G. Leyburn, *The Scotch-Irish: A Social History* (Chapel Hill, N.C., 1962); Helen H. Anderson, *Eden Prairie: The First 100 Years*, 21, 22, 28, 76–89 (Eden Prairie, 1979); Mary Jane Hill Anderson, *Autobiography of Mary Jane Hill Anderson, Wife of Robert Anderson*, 3–17, 29–35, 36 (Minneapolis, 1934); 1880 U.S. manuscript census schedules; Todd County Bicentennial Committee, *Todd County Histories*, 390–95 (Long Prairie, 1976); U.S., *Census, 1950, Population*, 23–52, and 1990, *Social and Economic Characteristics: Minnesota*, 67. The argument of Canadian historian Donald Akenson that there are far more Protestant Irish in the U.S. than have been acknowledged is not borne out in Minnesota. Donald Harman Akenson, *The Irish in Ontario: A Study in Rural History*, 346–49 (Montreal, 1984).

Potato Facts, p. 5: James S. Donnelly, Jr., *The Great Irish Potato Famine*, 1 (Gloucestershire, England, 2001); E. Margaret Crawford, "Food and Famine," in Cathal Póirteír, ed., *The Great Irish Famine*, 60 (Dublin, 1995).

A Farmer-Entrepreneur, p. 11: Letter in Michael Callahan and Family Papers, MHS; interview with Jack Callahan, Nov. 29, 2002.

The Sisters and the Schools, p. 21: Carol K. Coburn and Martha Smith, *Spirited Lives: How Nuns Shaped Catholic Culture and American Life, 1836–1920*, 53, 87–91, 129–31 (Chapel Hill, 1999); Suellen Hoy, "Women Religious from Ireland," in *Encylopedia of the Irish in America*, ed. Glazier, 971; phone interview with Sister Karen Kennelly, Nov. 12, 2001; "Sisters who entered the Sisters of St. Joseph of Carondelet from Ireland," compiled by Miriam Shea, CSJ, and Grace Saumur, CSJ, March 2001, copy in People of Minnesota Project Papers, MHS; Helen Angela Hurley, *On Good Ground*, 144, 265 (Minneapolis, 1951); Sister Karen Kennelly, CSJ, "The Dynamic Sister Antonia and the College of St. Catherine," in *Ramsey County History* 14: 3–18 (1978) (quotations p. 11, 16).

The Fifth Minnesota Regiment, p. 31: John D. Hicks, "The Organization of the Volunteer Army in 1861 with Special Reference to Minnesota," in *Minnesota History*, 2: 345–46 (Feb. 1918); Kenneth L. Carley, *Minnesota in the Civil War: An Illustrated History*, 99, 102 (St. Paul, 2000).

Mary Molloy, Dressmaker, p. 34: Judith Jerde, "Mary Molloy: St. Paul's Extraordinary Dressmaker," in *Minnesota History*, 47: 93–99 (Fall 1980).

A St. Paul Writer, p. 38: Mary Jo Tate, "F. Scott Fitzgerald," in Glazier, ed., *Encyclopedia of the Irish in America*, 331.

Irish Boxers, p. 49: Minneapolis Journal, Jan. 19, 1887; *St. Paul Pioneer Press*, July 5, 1923, p. 1, July 29, 2001, p. 1; *Irish Gazette*, Jan./Feb. 1998, p. 4; *St. Paul Dispatch*, April 17 and 18, 1936, both p. 6.

The Other Sullivans, p. 53: Star Tribune, June 26, 2001, p. 1.

From Irish Farm to Suburb, p. 55: Articles by Joe Sullivan in *St. Patrick's News-Net* (Edina), Feb., Apr., Sept., Nov. 1996,

Sept. 1997, and May 1998, and in *Irish Gazette*, Oct. 1999, p. 8; Deborah Morse-Kahn, *Chapters in the City History: Edina,* 10, 14, 16, 69, 71, 106 ([Edina], 1988).

The MacBride Principles, p. 59: Star Tribune, Feb. 15, 1988, Feb. 16, 1988, p. 11A, Feb. 17, 1988, p. 3B; *St. Paul Pioneer Press Dispatch,* June 7, 1987, 1H, Sept. 21, 1987, 7A, Jan. 21, 1988, p. 2G; Mar. 9, 1988, p. 12A, Mar. 11, 1988, p. 8A; *Irish Echo* (New York), Apr. 30, 1988, p. 1.

Index

Page numbers in italic refer to pictures and captions.

Picture Credits

Names of the photographers, when known, are in parentheses following the page number on which the picture appears.

Minnesota Historical Society—page x, 8 (John Runk), 10, 12 (both; top, William Sharkey), 13 (both; top, Amasa A. Houghton), 14, 15, 17, 18 (Golling Studio), 20, 24, 25 (both), 26 (B. F. Childs), 28, 29, 31, 33, 34, 35, 37 (A. Irber), 38, 39, 40 (both), 42 (both; bottom, Shepherd), 43, 46, 49 (*Minneapolis Tribune*), 52, 53 (*Minneapolis Tribune*), 55, 57 (both), 59, 61 (Mike Fitzgerald), 62, 64 (Steve Plattner), 65

Library of Congress, Washington, D.C.—cover (John Vachon), 16 (both, John Vachon)

Sisters of St. Joseph, St. Paul—page 21

Leah Curtin—page 63 (both)

Ann Gigrich—page 68

Acknowledgments

The author wishes to thank Francis Carroll, Daniel Larmouth, Virginia McBride, Ben Petry, Shana Redmond, Sally Rubinstein, James Rogers, Bruce White, and Mary Lethert Wingerd for their assistance.

Minnesotans can trace their families and their state's heritage to a multitude of ethnic groups. *The People of Minnesota* series tells each group's story in a compact, handsomely illustrated, and accessible paperback. Readers will learn about the group's accomplishments, ethnic organizations, settlement patterns, and occupations. Each book includes a personal story of one person or family, told through a diary, a letter, or an oral history.

In his introduction to the series, Bill Holm reminds us why these stories are as important as ever: "To be ethnic, somehow, is to be human. Neither can we escape it, nor should we want to. You cannot interest yourself in the lives of your neighbors if you don't take sufficient interest in your own."

This series is based on the critically acclaimed book *They Chose Minnesota: A Survey of the State's Ethnic Groups* (Minnesota Historical Society Press). The volumes in *The People of Minnesota* bring each group's story up to date and add dozens of photographs to inform and enhance the telling.

Books in the series include *Irish in Minnesota, Jews in Minnesota, Norwegians in Minnesota,* and *African Americans in Minnesota.*

Bill Holm is the grandson of four Icelandic immigrants to Minneota, Minnesota, where he still lives. He is the author of eight books including *Eccentric Island: Travels Real and Imaginary* and *Coming Home Crazy.* When he is not practicing the piano or on the road circuit-riding for literature, he teaches at Southwest State University in Marshall, Minnesota.

About the Author

Ann Regan is the managing editor of the Minnesota Historical Society Press. She authored the original chapter on the Irish in *They Chose Minnesota.*